The Far Side Observer

Other Books in The Far Side Series

The Far Side
Beyond The Far Side
In Search of The Far Side
Bride of The Far Side
Valley of The Far Side
It Came From The Far Side
Hound of The Far Side

Anthologies

The Far Side Gallery
The Far Side Gallery 2

The Far Side Observer

BY GARY LARSON

Andrews and McMeel
A Universal Press Syndicate Company
Kansas City • New York

For information write Andrews and McMeel, a Universal Press Syndicate Company, 4900 Main Street, Kansas City, Missouri 64112.

ISBN: 0-8362-2098-6
Library of Congress Catalog Card Number: 87-71161

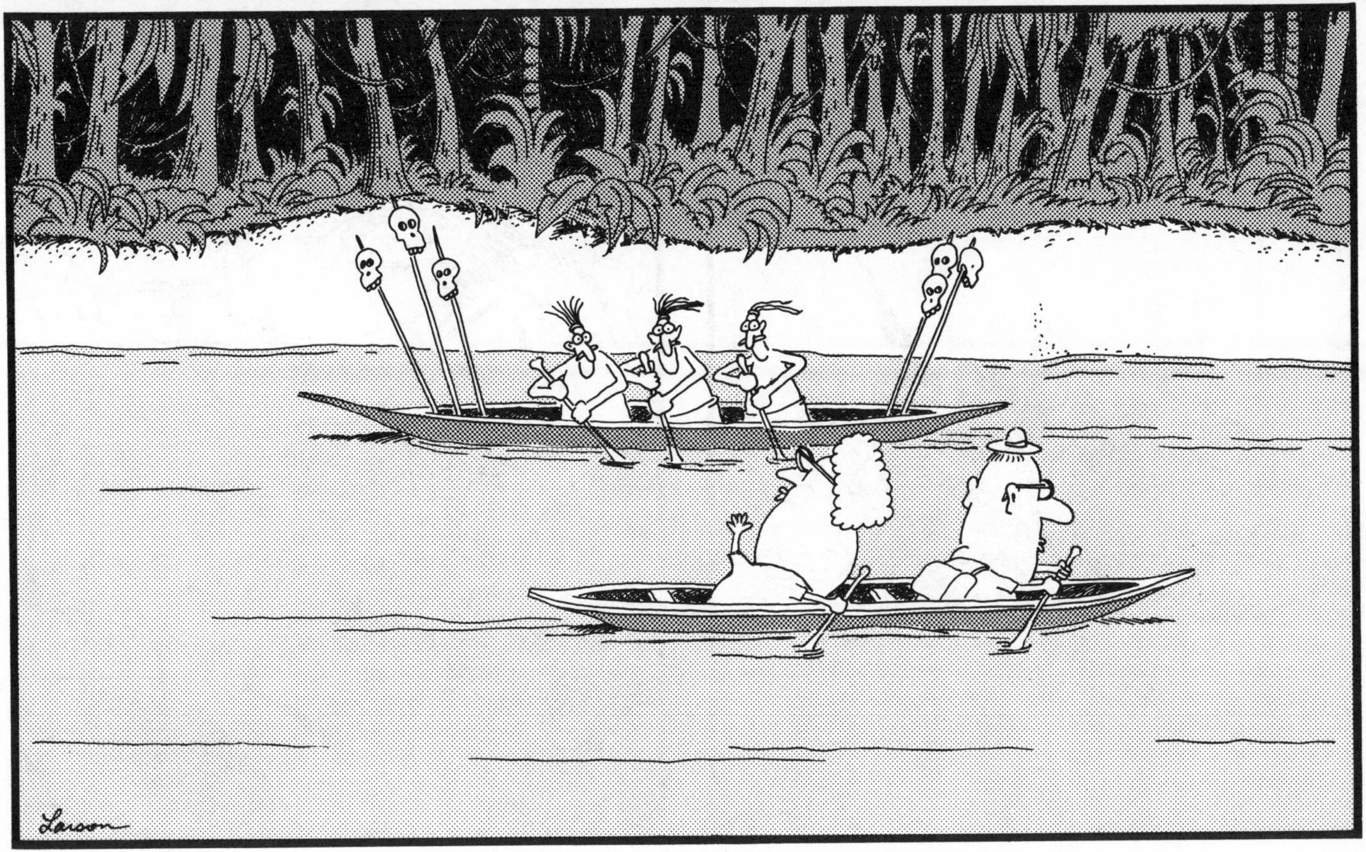
Larson

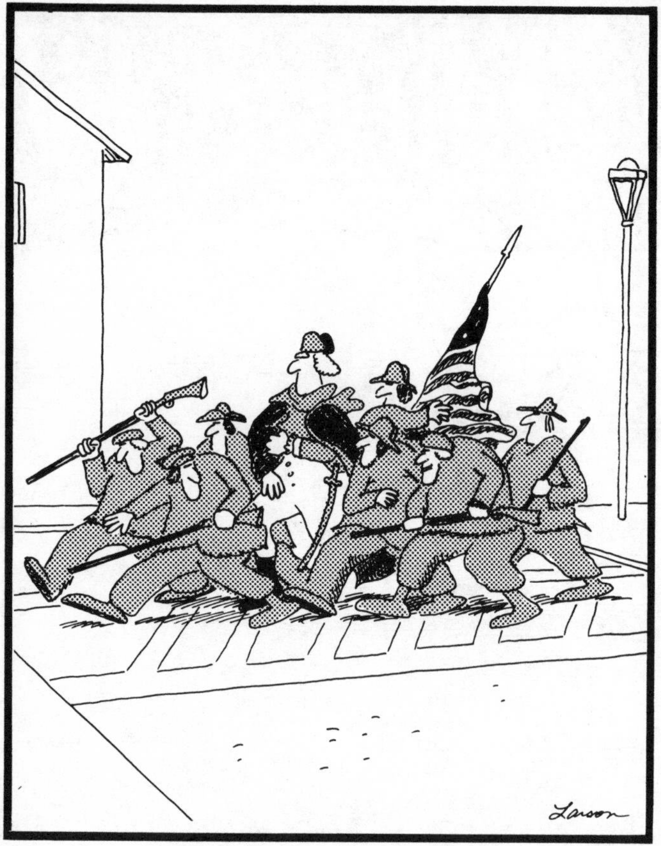
Larson

Washington crossing the street

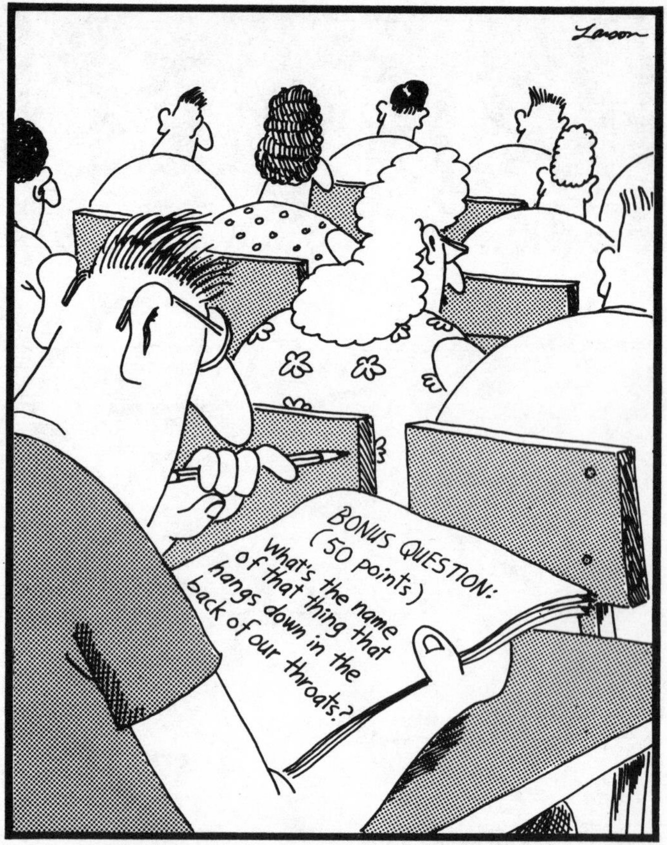
Larson
BONUS QUESTION:
(50 points)
What's the name
of that thing that
hangs down in the
back of our throats?

Final page of the Medical Boards

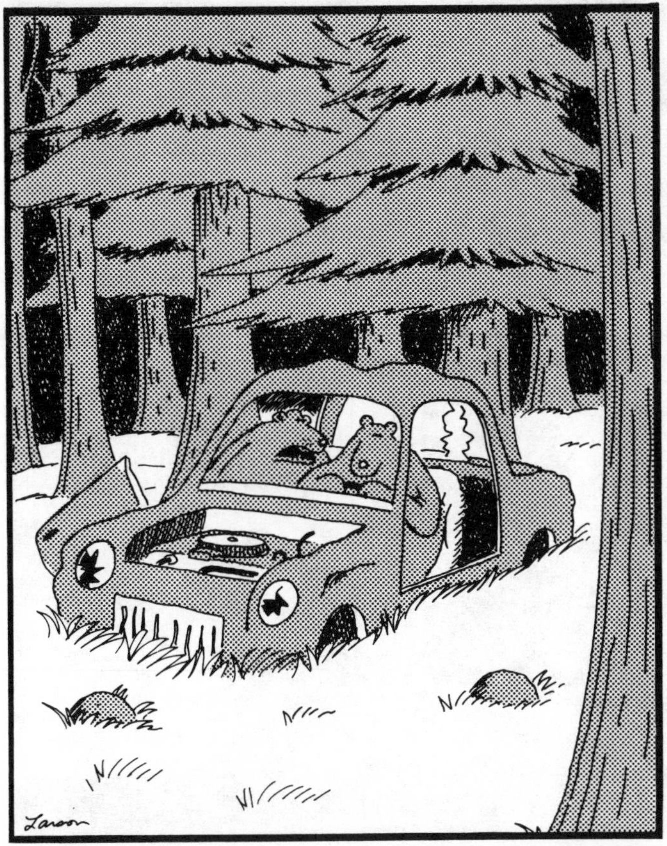
Larson

"Think about it, Murray. ... If we could get this baby runnin', we could run over hikers, pick up females, chase down mule deer — man, we'd be the grizzlies from hell."

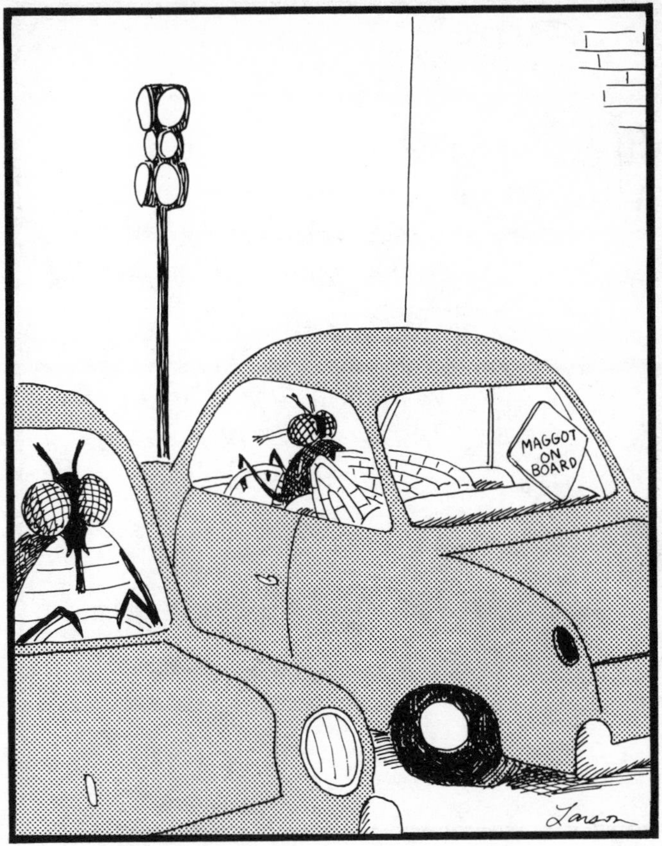
MAGGOT
ON
BOARD
Larson

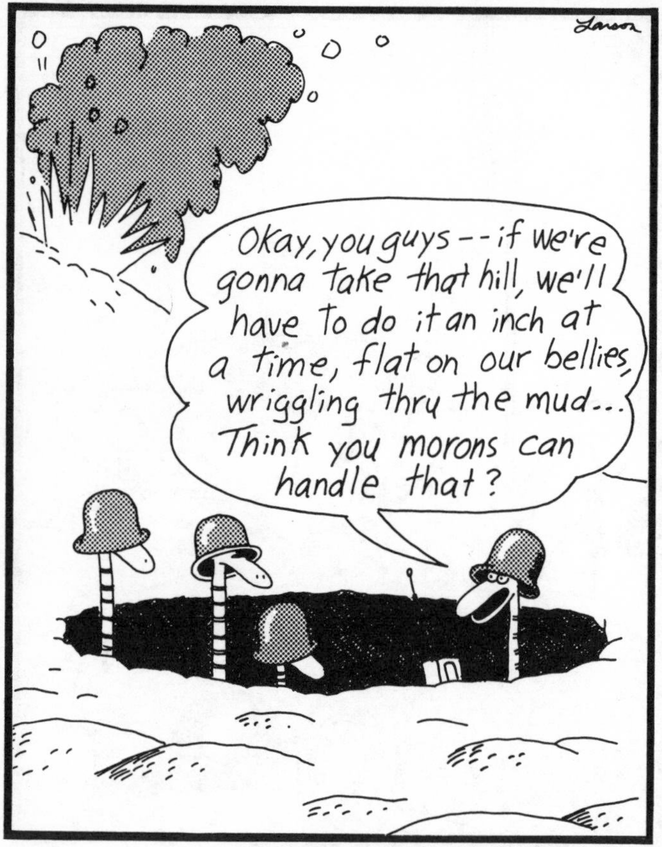
Larson
Okay, you guys -- if we're gonna take that hill, we'll have to do it an inch at a time, flat on our bellies, wriggling thru the mud... Think you morons can handle that?

The Snakes of War

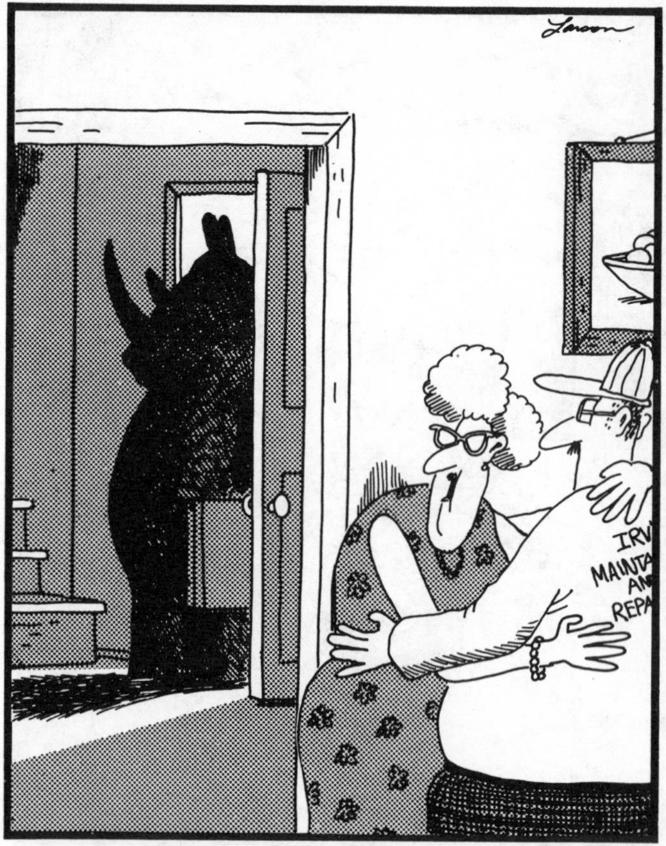
Larson

"My God! Willard's home early! Don't move — his vision's not very good, but his sense of smell and hearing are quite acute."

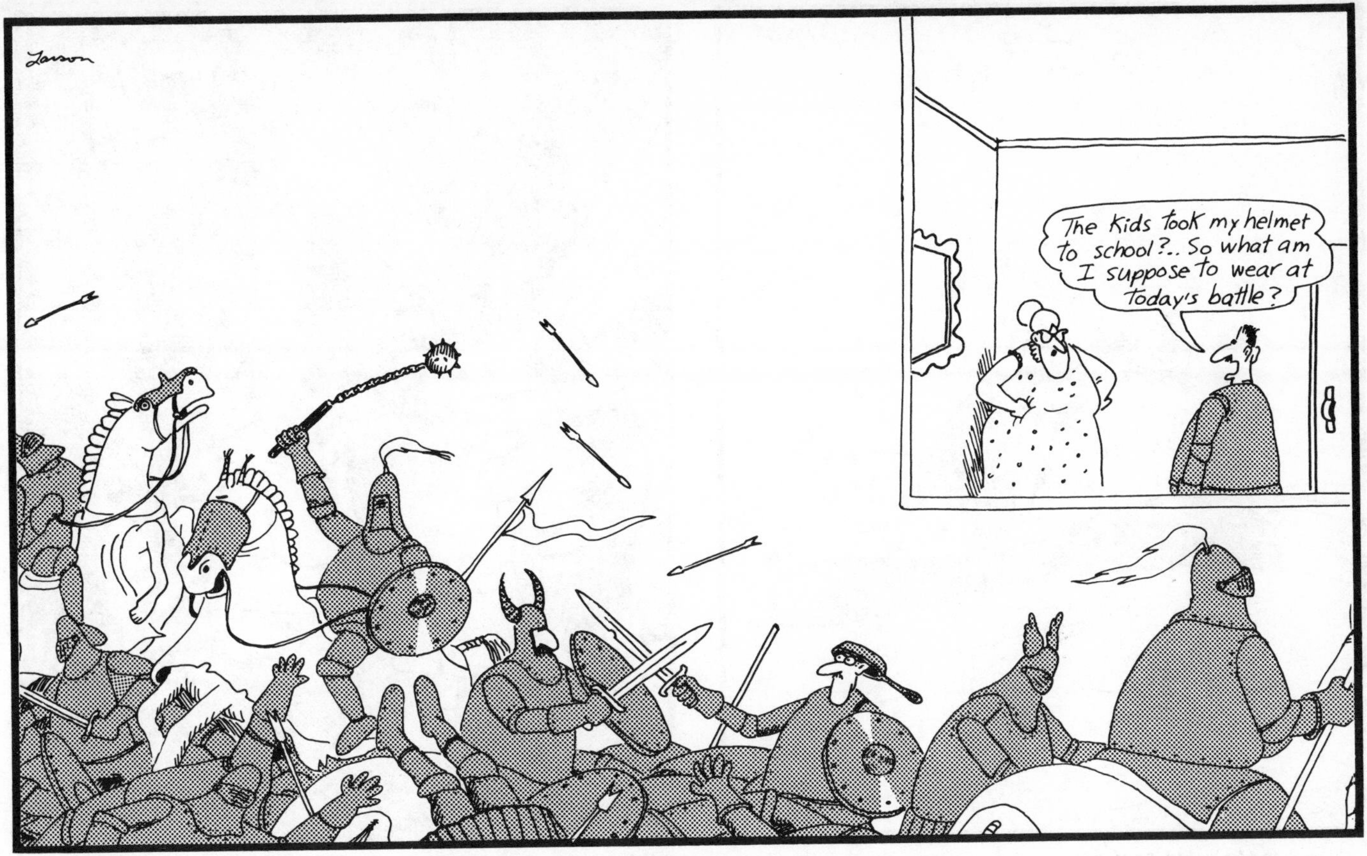
Larson
The kids took my helmet to school?.. So what am I suppose to wear at today's battle?

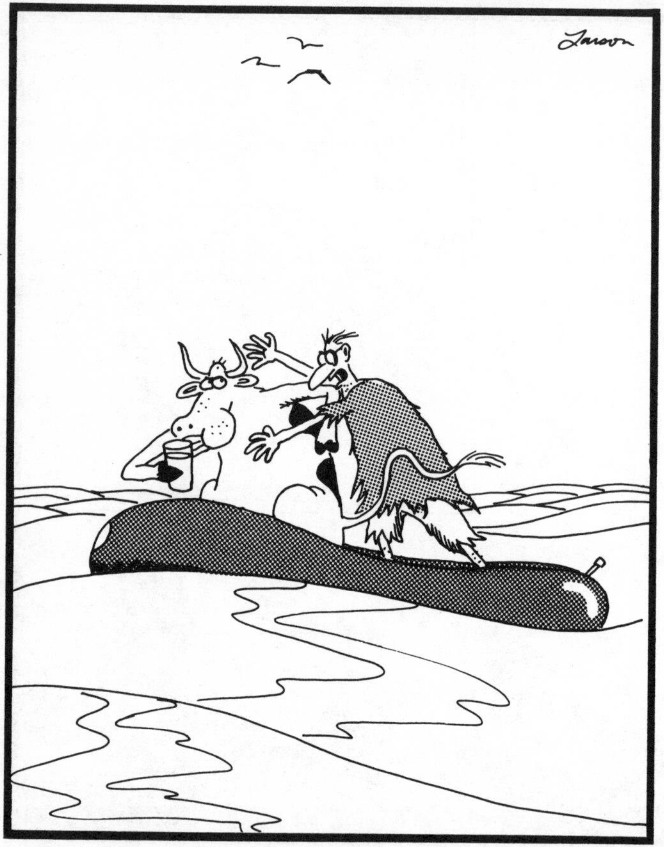

"Hey! That's milk! And you said you were all empty, you stinkin' liar!"

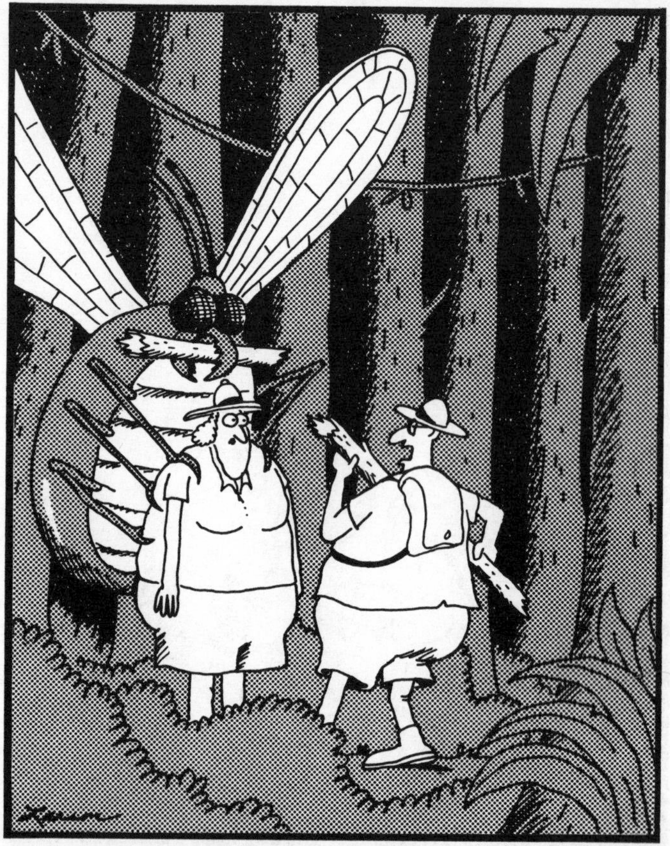

"Holy moley, Loretta! Not only is it still there, look what it did to the end of my stick!"

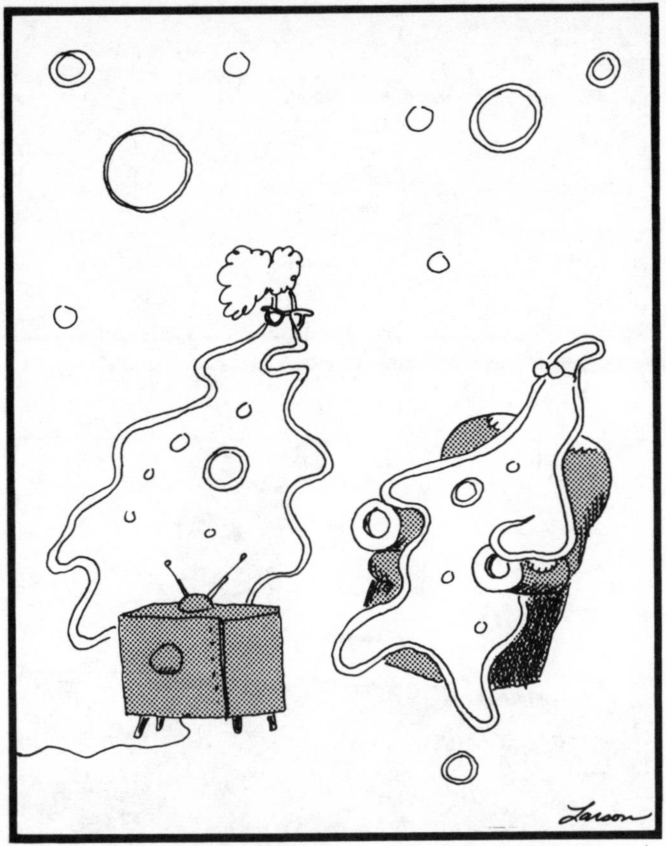
Larson

"Stimulus, response! Stimulus, response! Don't you ever *think*?"

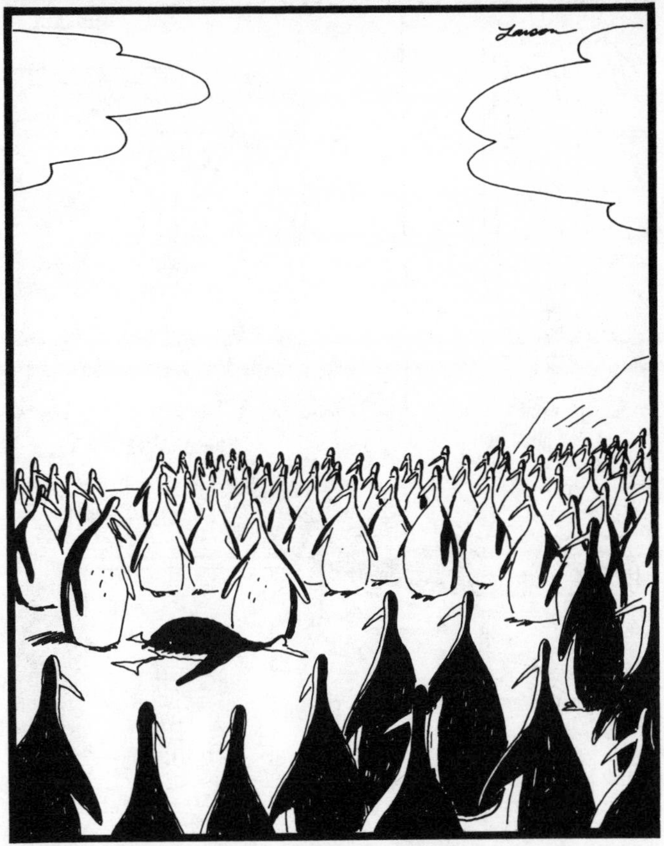
Larson

"He's dead, all right — beaked in the back . . . and, you know, this won't be easy to solve."

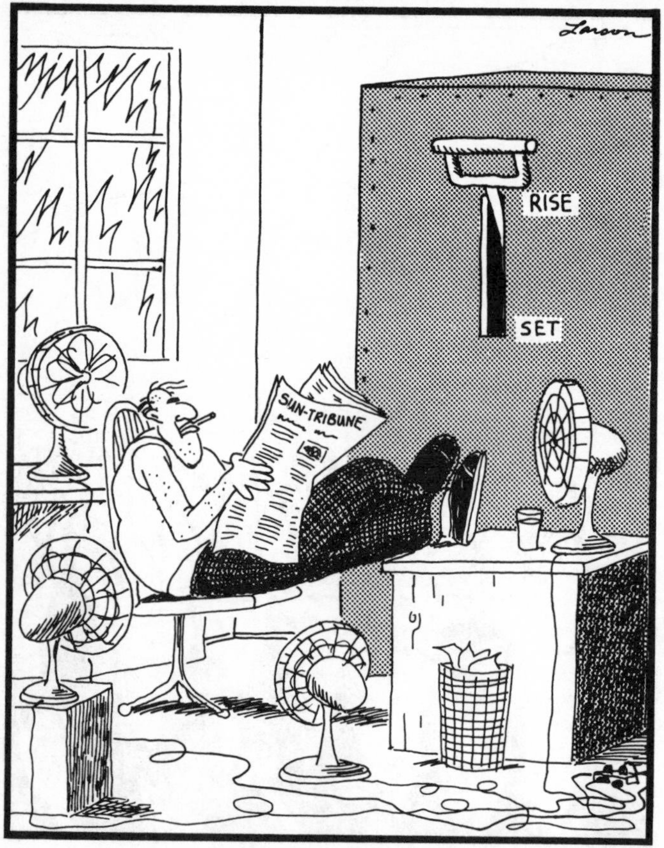
Larson
RISE
SET
SUN-TRIBUNE

Inside the sun

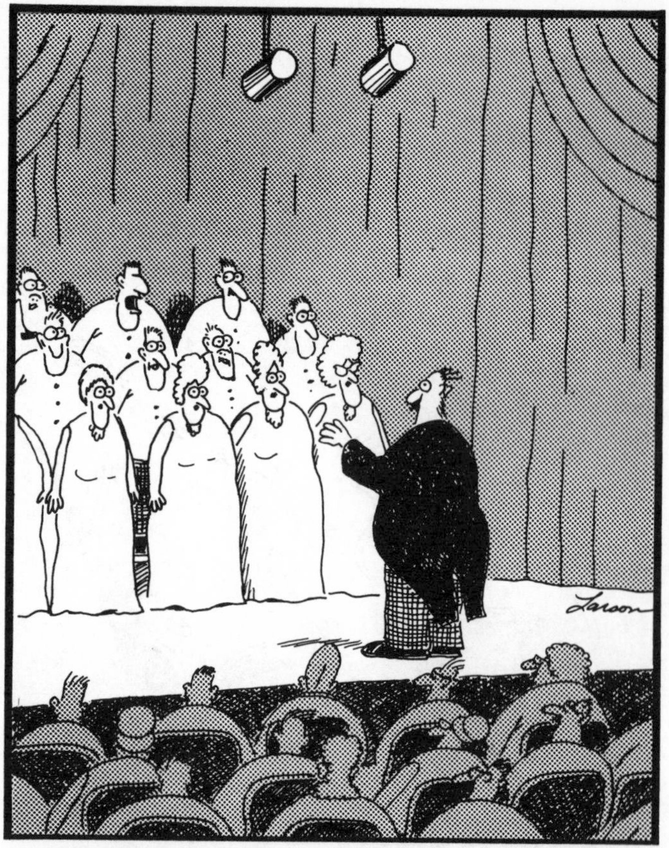
Larson

In that one split second, when the choir's last note had ended, but before the audience could respond, Vinnie Conswego belches the phrase, "That's all, folks."

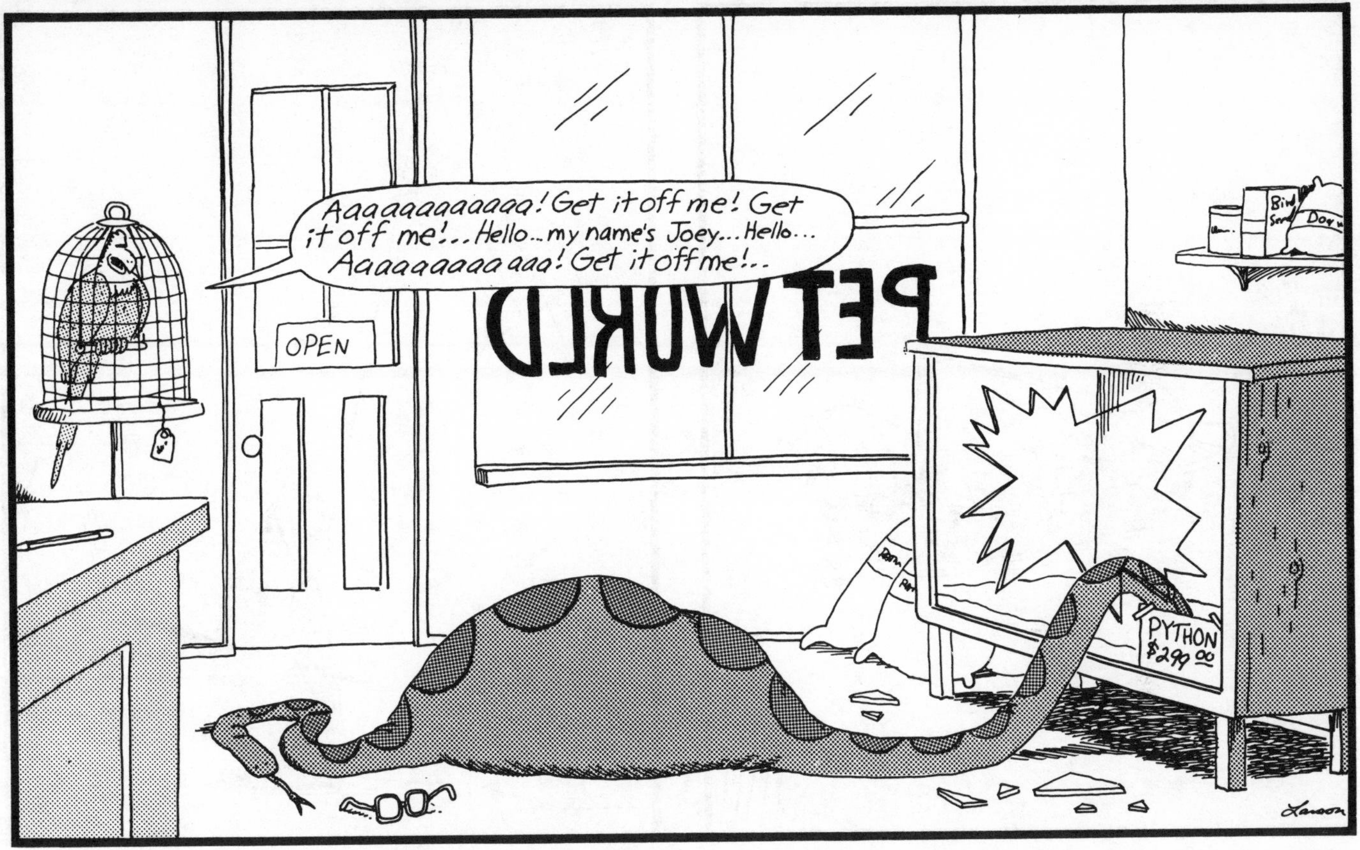
Aaaaaaaaaaaa! Get it off me! Get it off me!.. Hello... my name's Joey... Hello... Aaaaaaaaaaaa! Get it off me!..
OPEN
PET WORLD
PYTHON $299.00
Larson

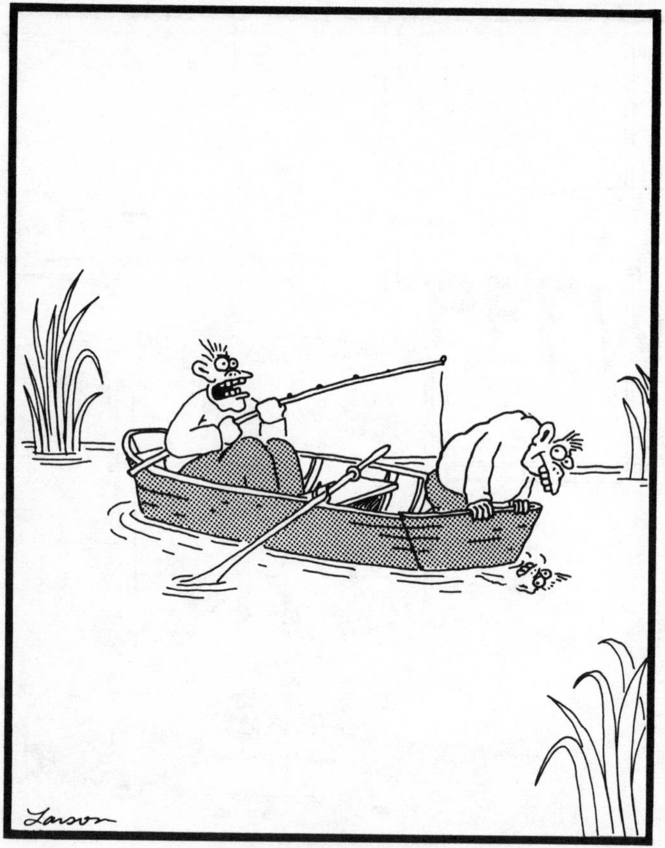
Larson

"Allen, you jerk! Dad told us not to do that or we'd scare the fish!"

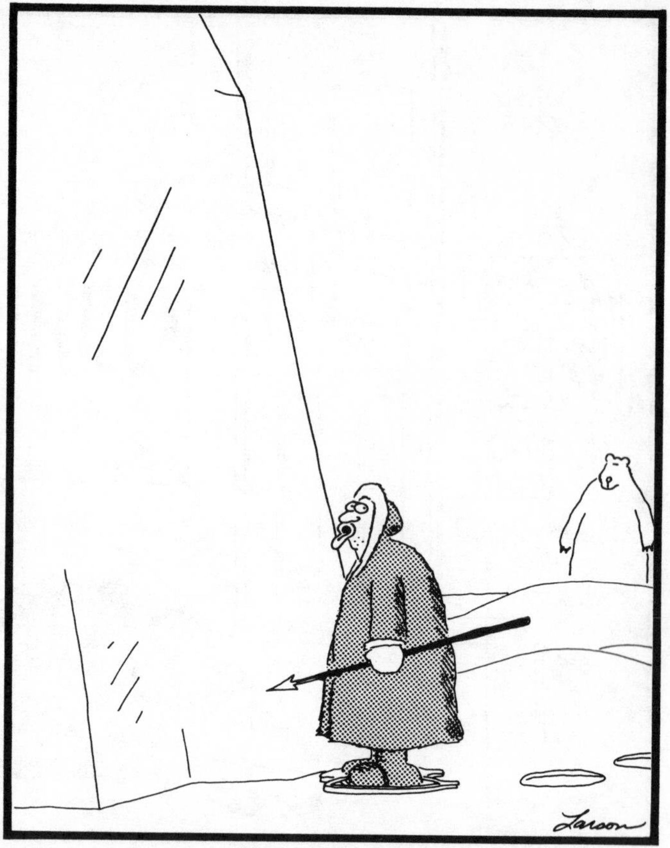
Larson

Never put your tongue on a glacier.

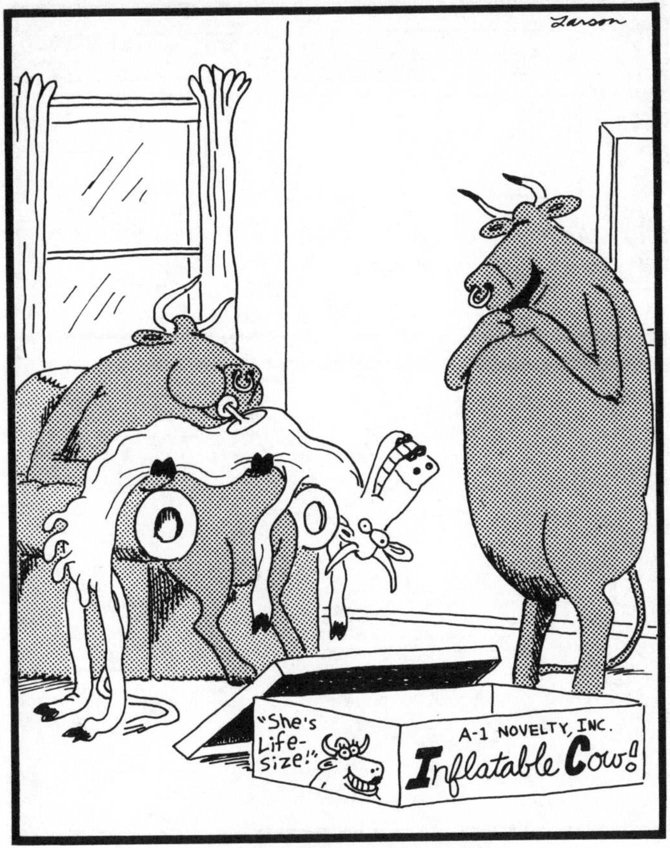
Larson
"She's Life-size!"
A-1 NOVELTY, INC.
Inflatable Cow!

"She's lookin' good, Vern!"

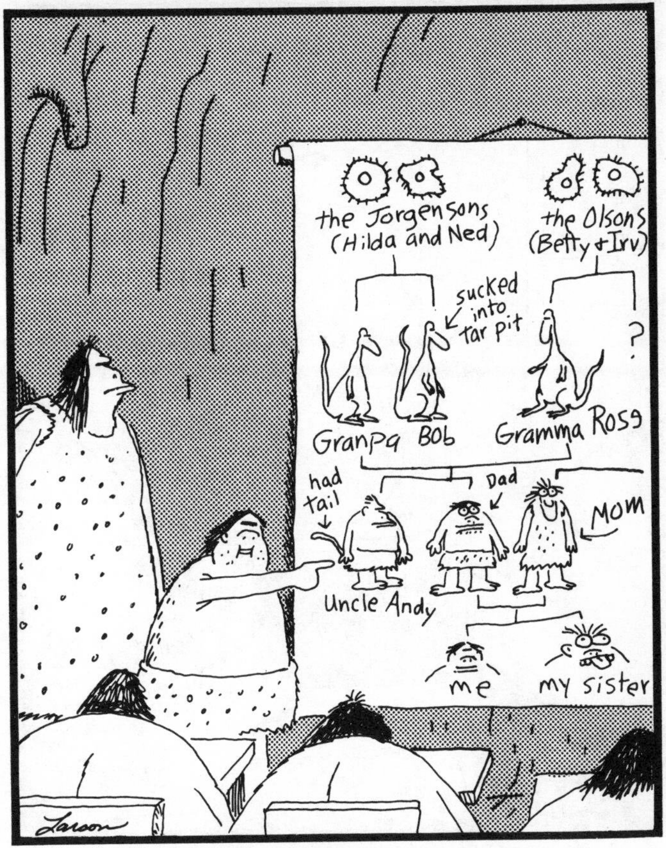
the Jorgensons
(Hilda and Ned)
the Olsons
(Betty + Irv)
sucked into tar pit
?
Granpa
Bob
Gramma Rose
had tail
Dad
MOM
Uncle Andy
me
my sister
Larson

Dirk brings his family tree to class.

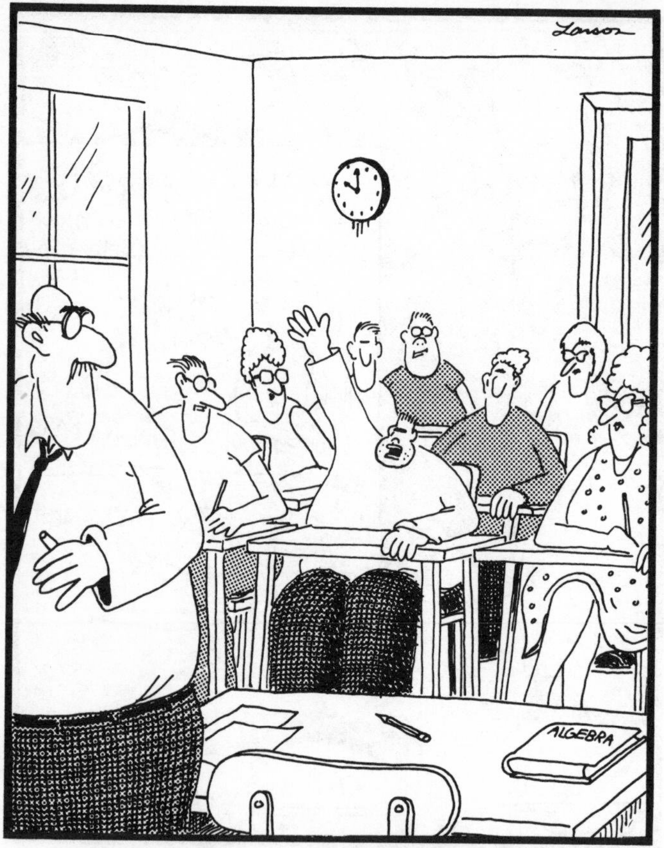
Larson
ALGEBRA

"Mr. Osborne, may I be excused? My brain is full."

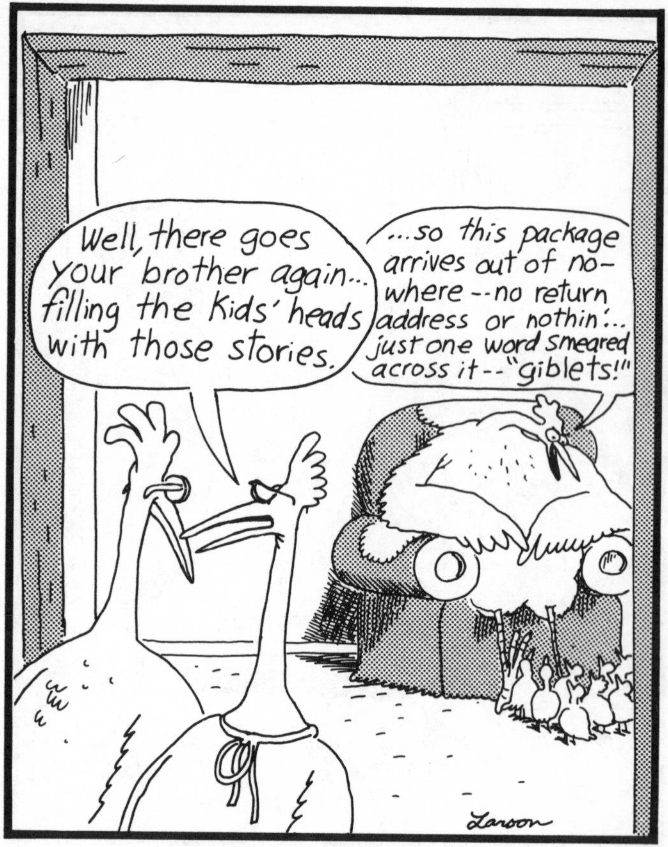
Well, there goes your brother again... filling the kids' heads with those stories.
...so this package arrives out of nowhere --no return address or nothin'... just one word smeared across it--"giblets!"
Larson

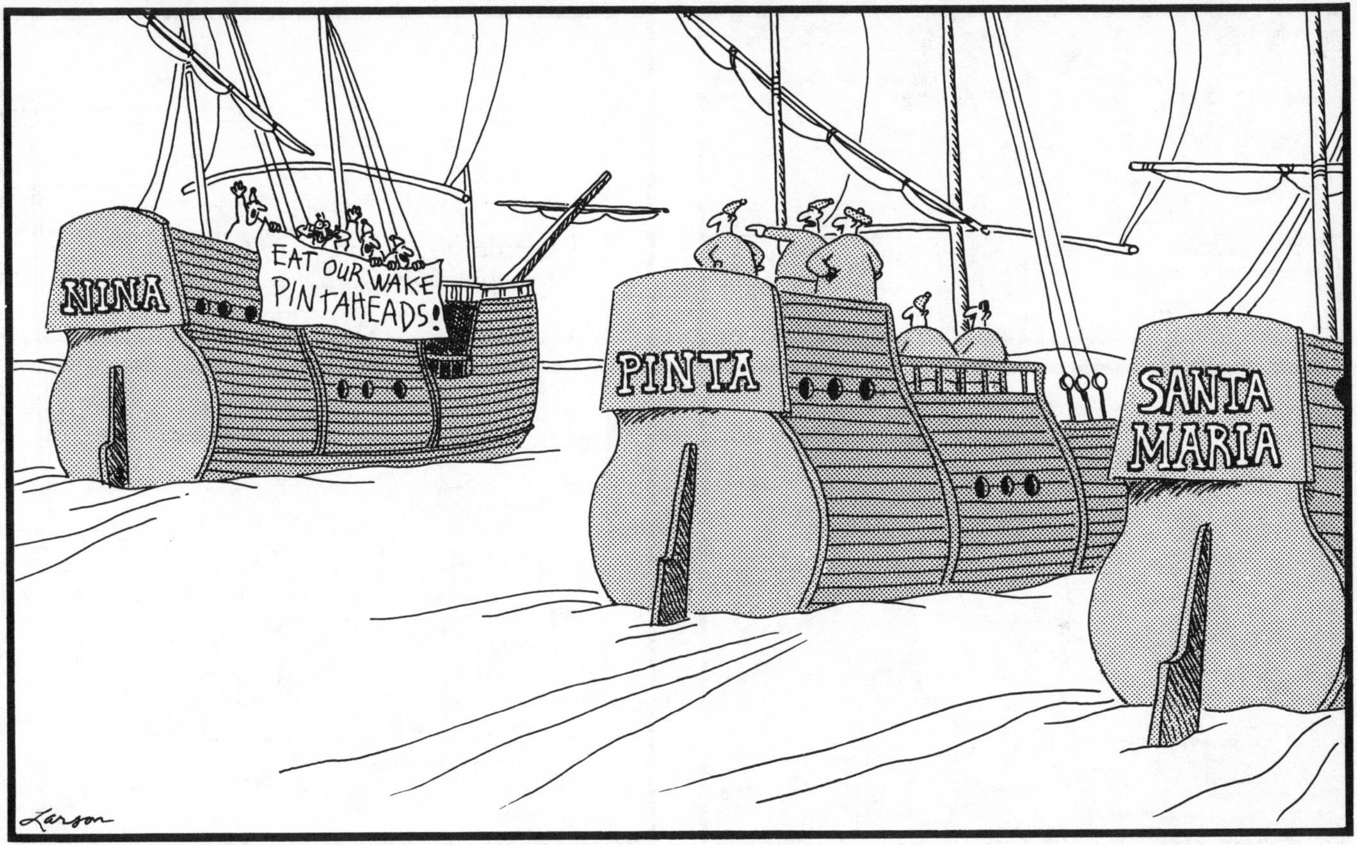
NINA
EAT OUR WAKE PINTAHEADS!
PINTA
SANTA MARIA
Larson

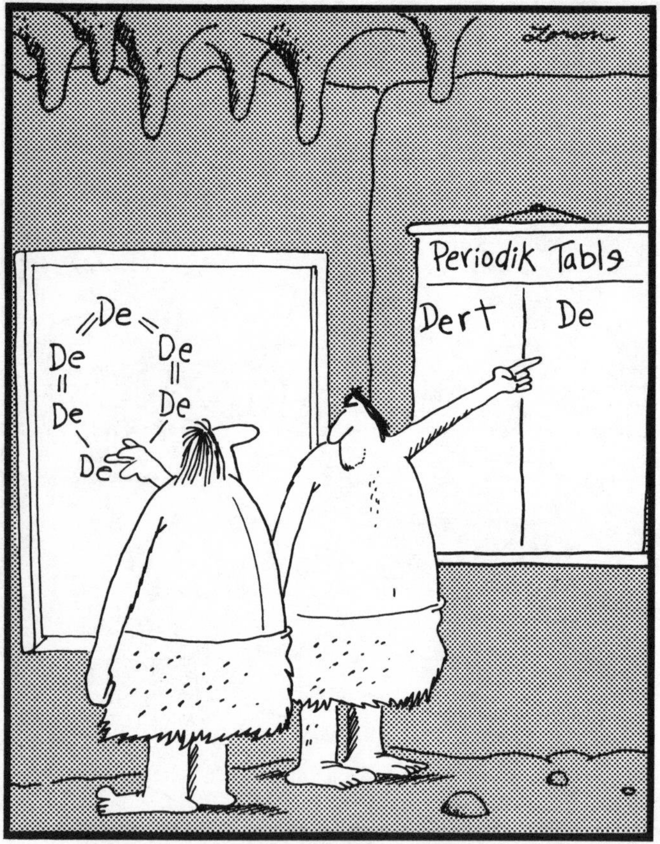
Larson
Periodik Tabl9
Dert
De
De
De
De
De
De
De

Early chemists describe the first dirt molecule.

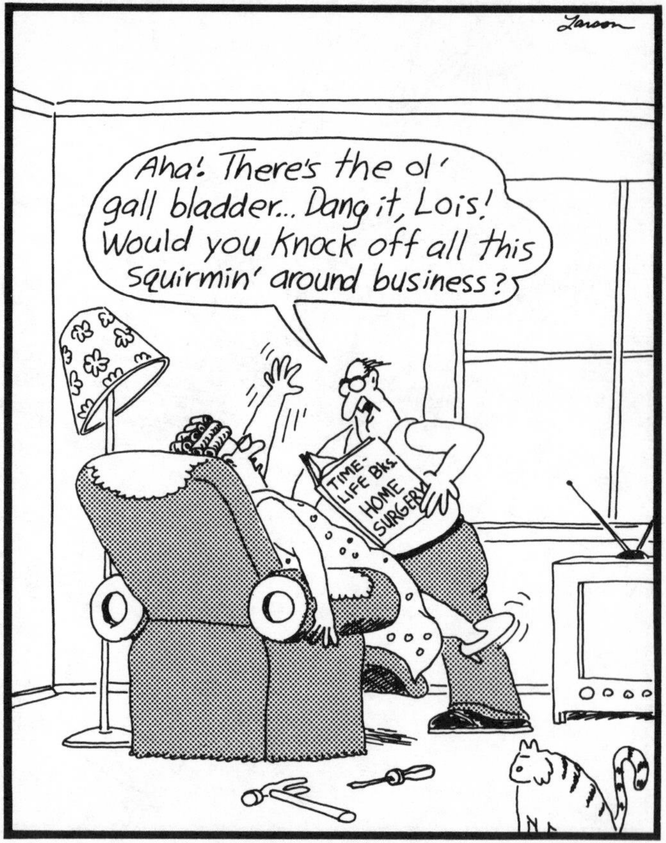
Larson
Aha! There's the ol' gall bladder... Dang it, Lois! Would you knock off all this squirmin' around business?
TIME-LIFE Bks HOME SURGERY

Volume five in a series

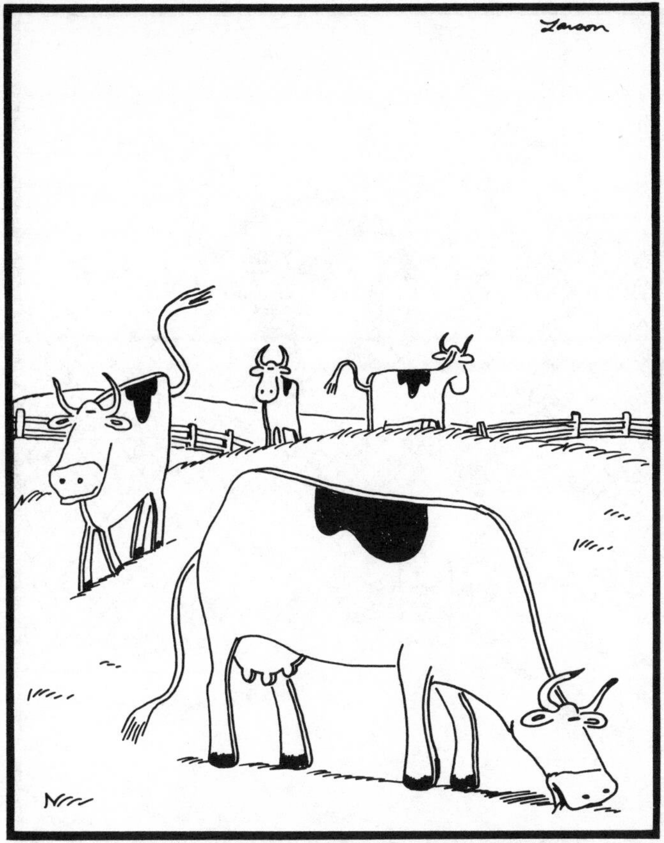
Larson

Where "minute" steaks come from

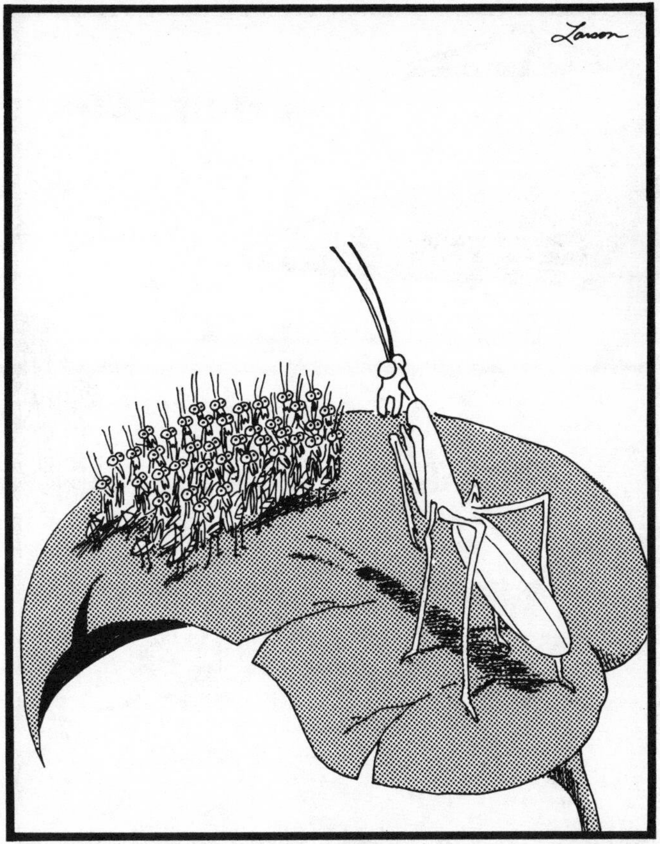
Larson

"Of course, long before you mature, most of you will be eaten."

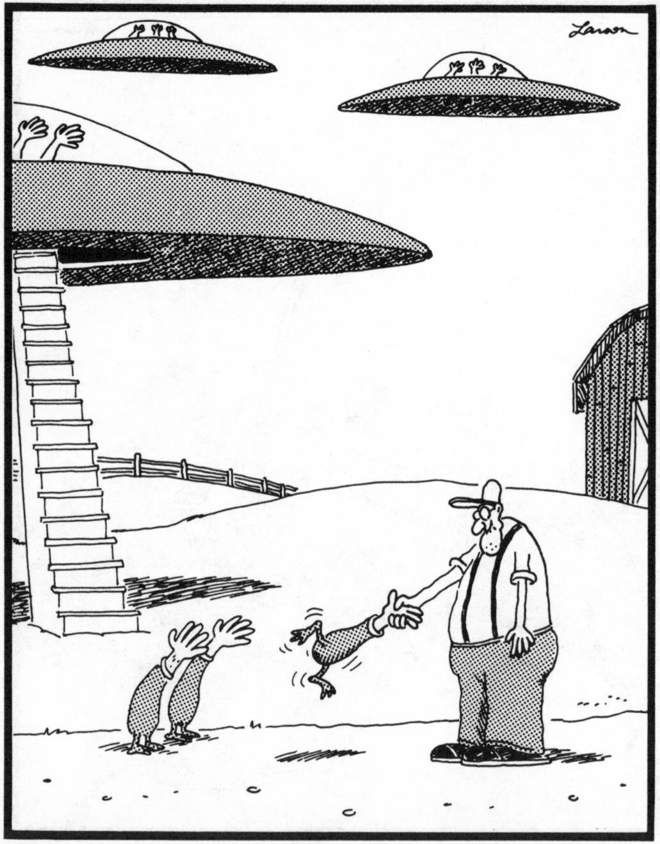

Larson

Inadvertently, Roy dooms the entire earth to annihilation when, in an attempt to be friendly, he seizes their leader by the head and shakes vigorously.

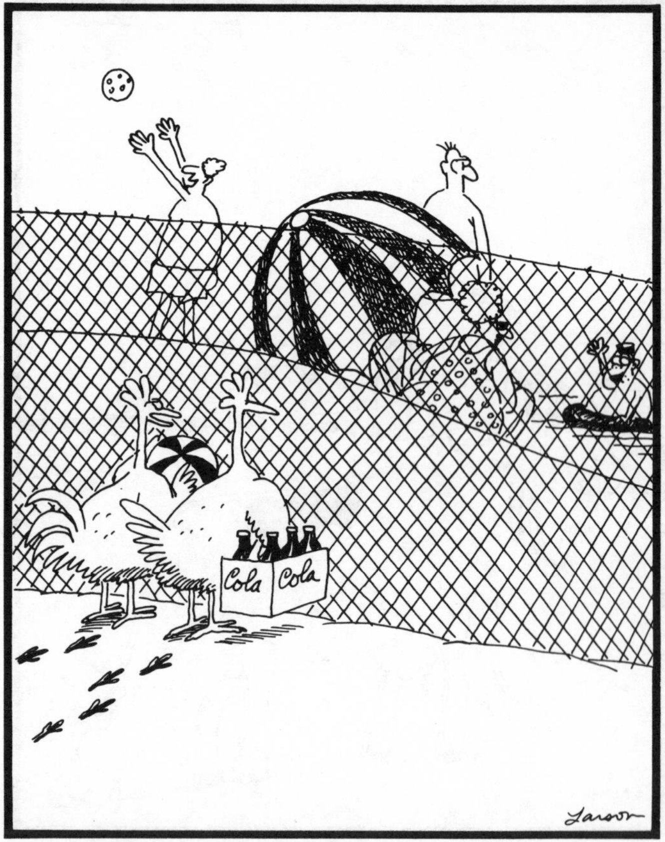

Cola
Cola
Larson

"Well, wouldn't you know it — we've come all this way to our favorite beach and someone's strung chicken wire around it."

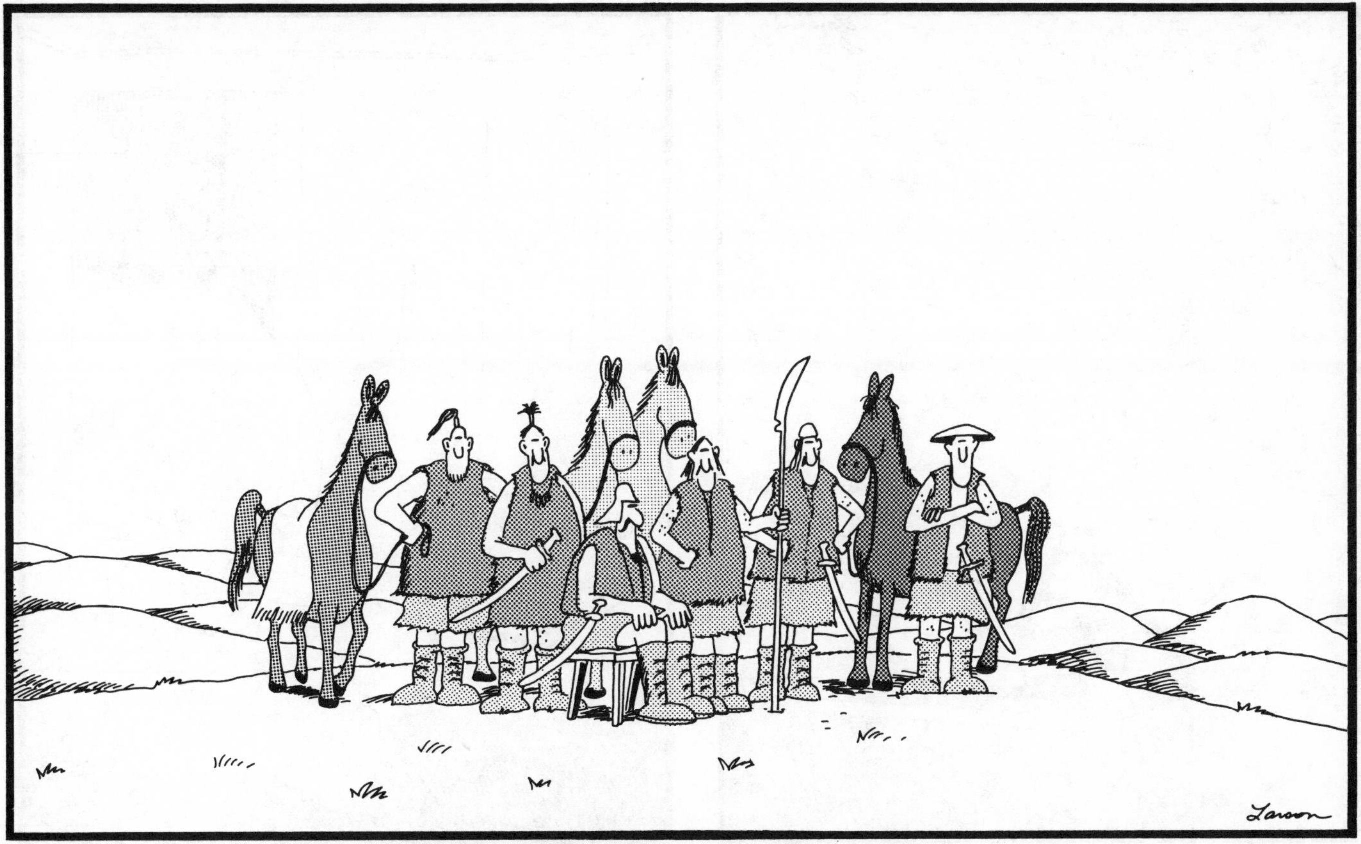
Larson

A young Genghis Khan and his Mongol hordette

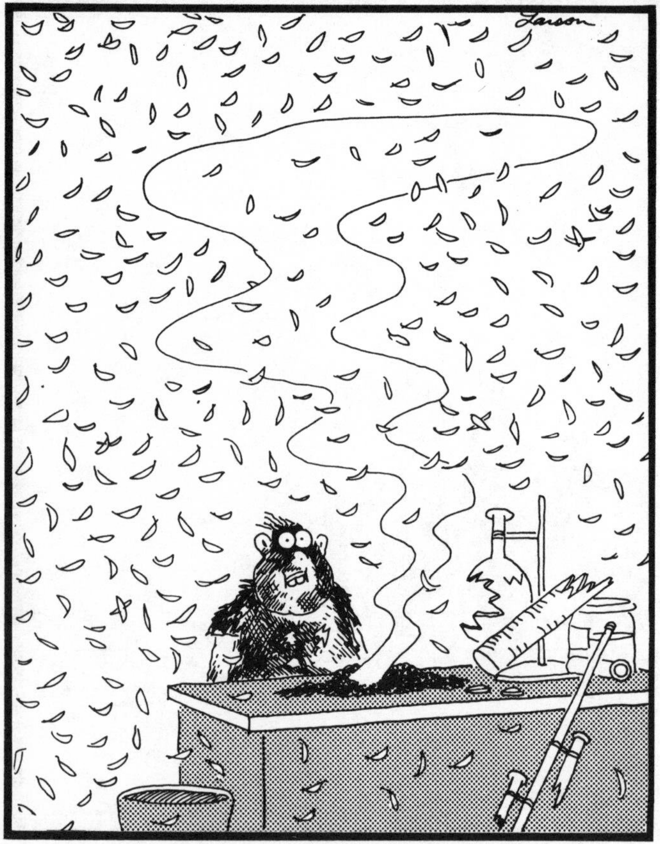
Larson

God as a kid tries to make a chicken in his room.

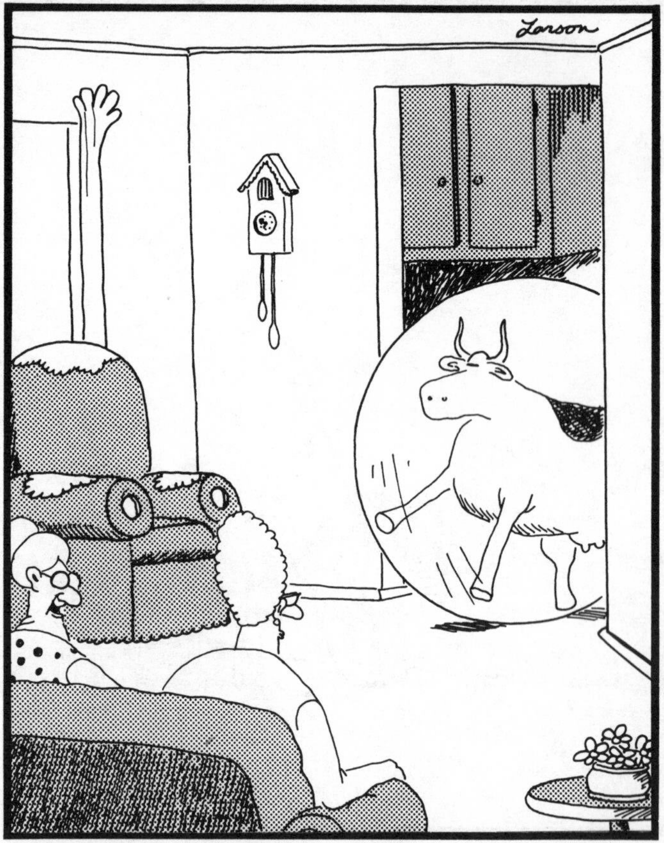
Larson

"Ooo! *This* is always amusing. . . . Here comes Bessie inside her plastic cow ball."

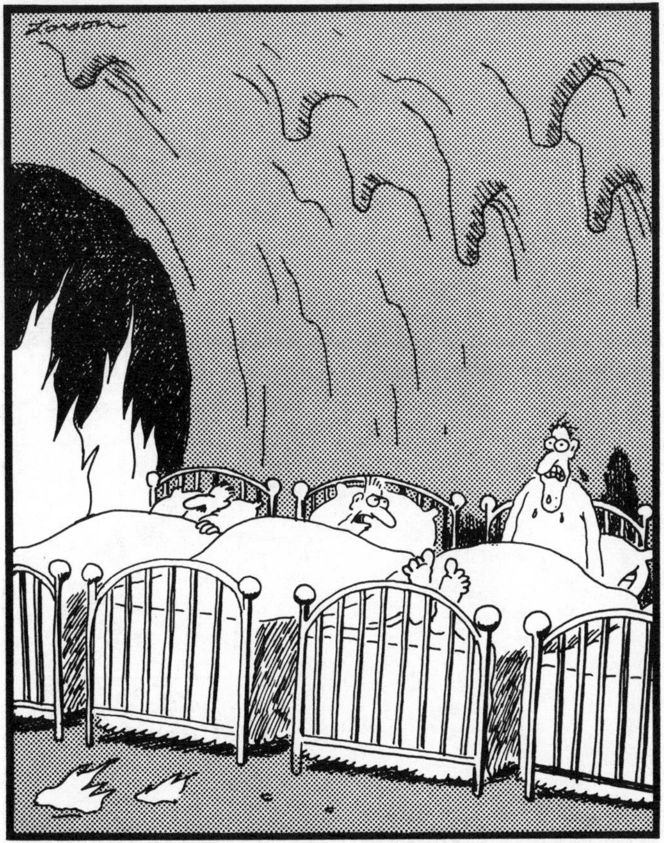
Larson

"Go back to sleep, Chuck. You're just havin' a nightmare — of course, we *are* still in hell."

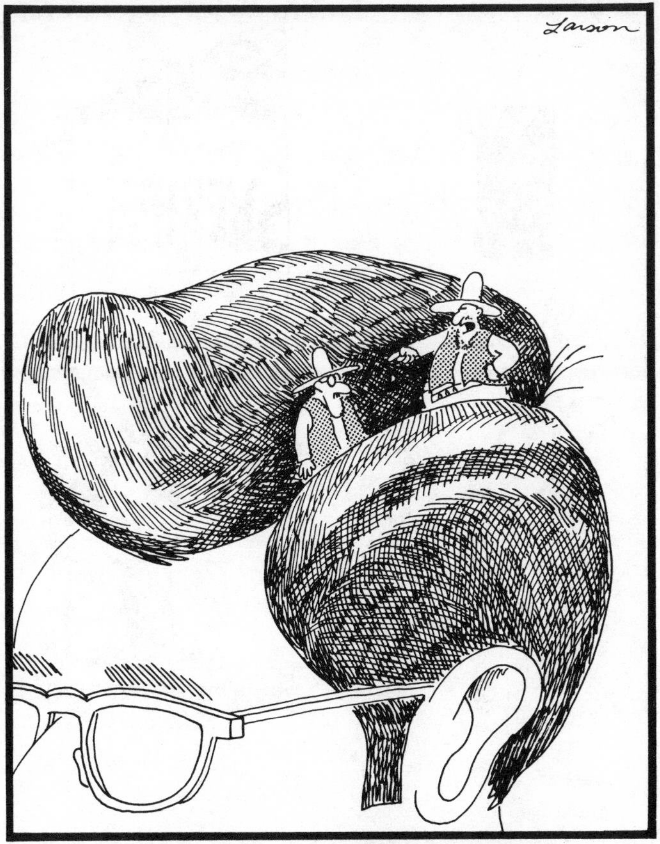
Larson

"Say, ain't you a stranger in this part?"

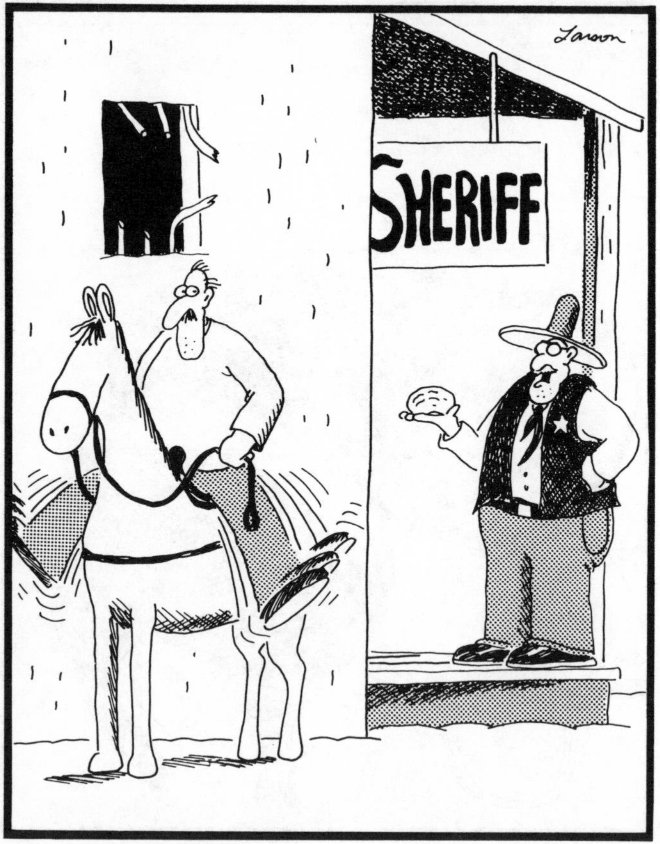
Larson
SHERIFF

"Ha! Figured you might try escapin', Bert — so I just took the liberty of removin' your horse's brain."

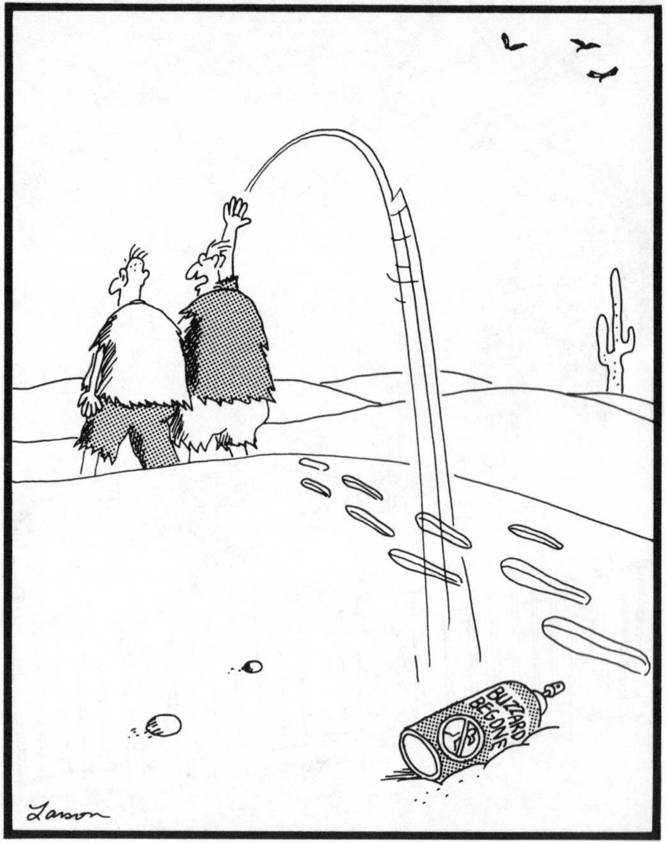
BUZZARD BEGONE
Larson

"And now that's the last of that."

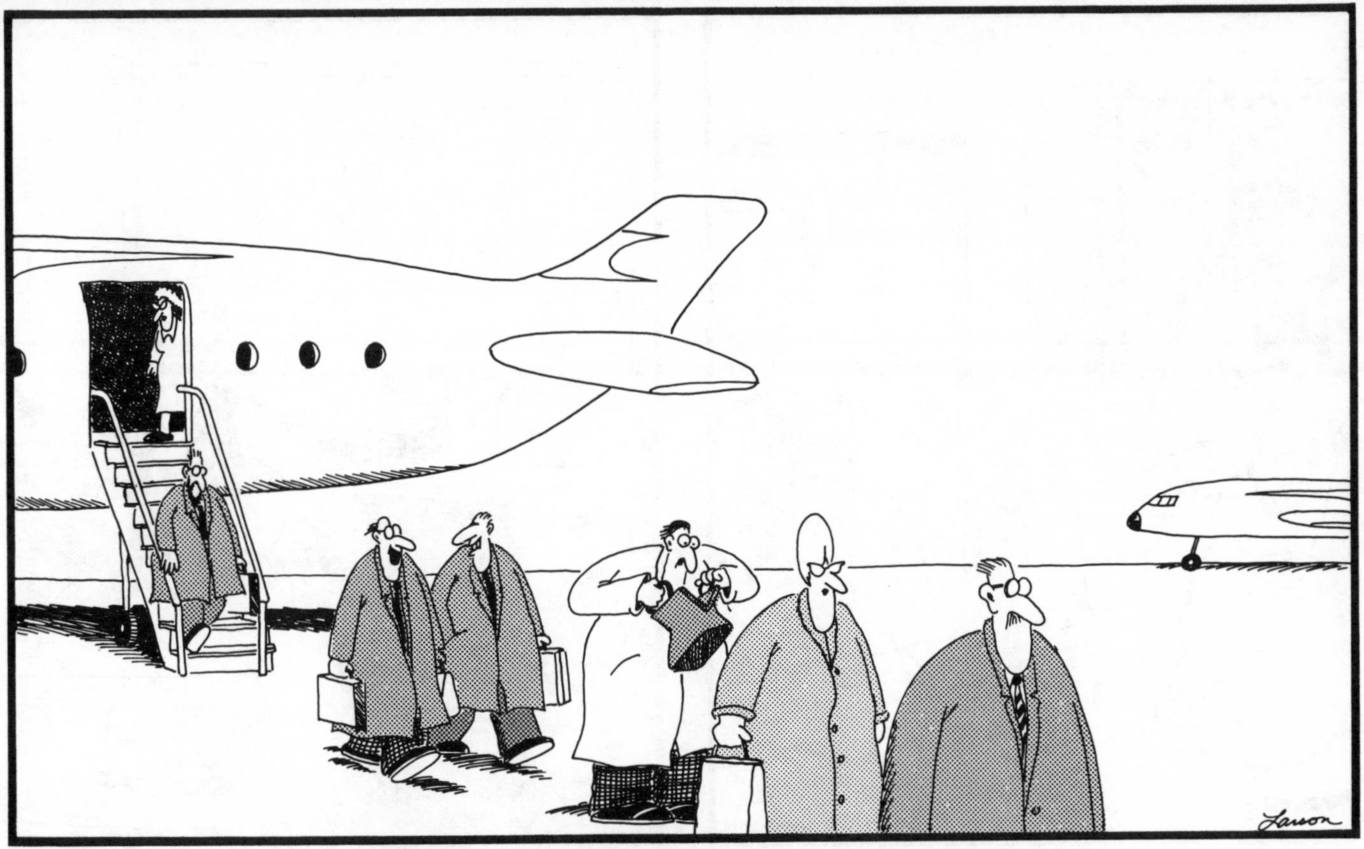
Larson

Suddenly, Dr. Frankenstein realized he had left his brain in San Francisco.

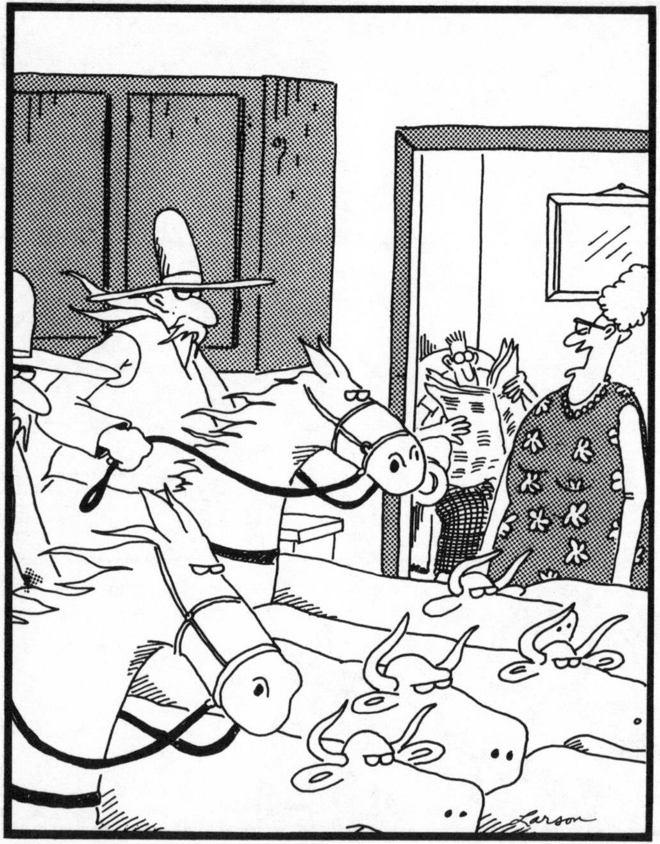
Larson

"Henry! Hurry or you're gonna miss it — ghost riders in the kitchen!"

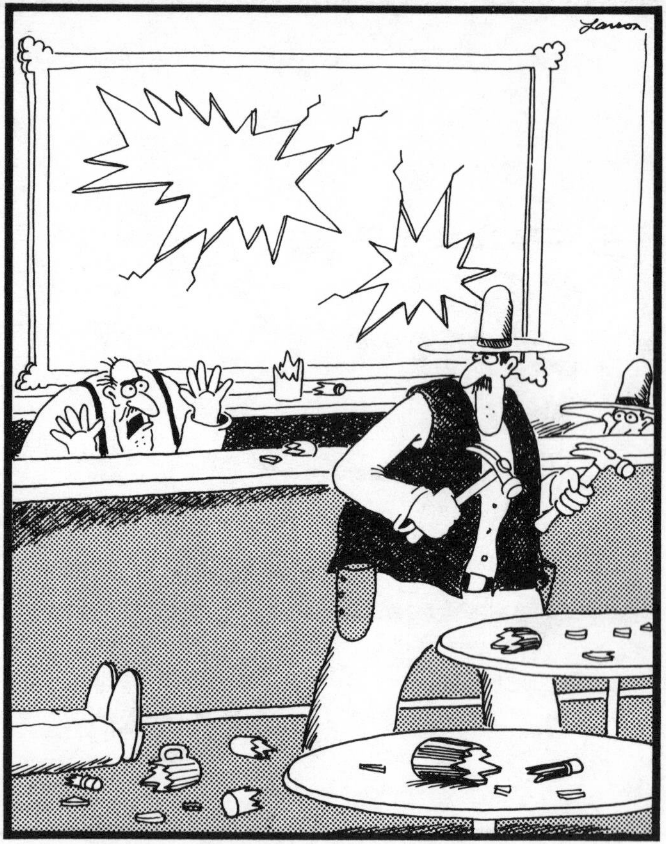
Larson

"Hey! C'mon, Jed! . . . Ease up on them hammers!"

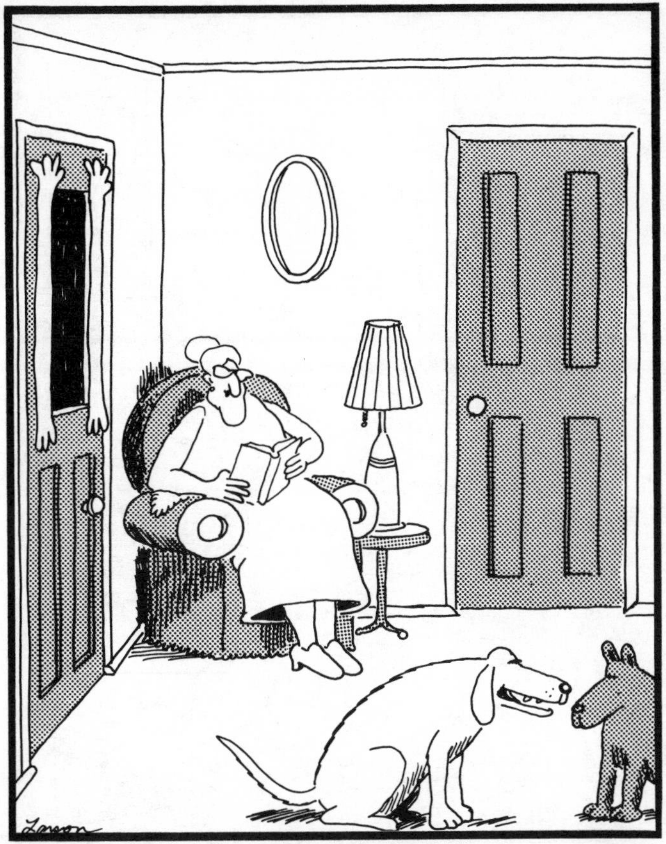
Larson

"You wanna have some fun, Fred? Watch . . . Growling and bristling, I'm gonna stand in front of the closet door and just stare."

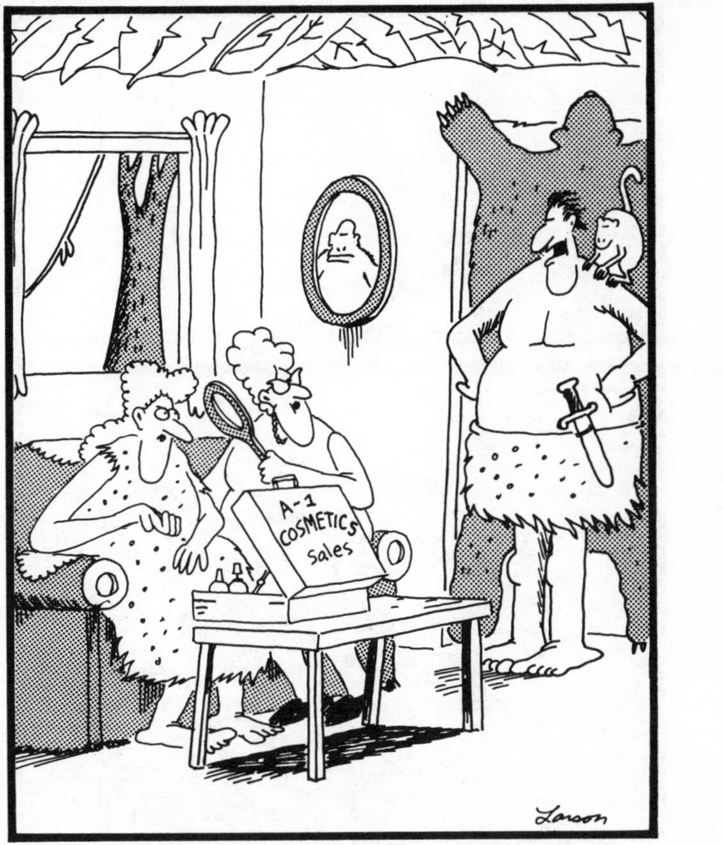
A-1
COSMETICS
Sales
Larson

"Whoa! Smells like a French primate house in here."

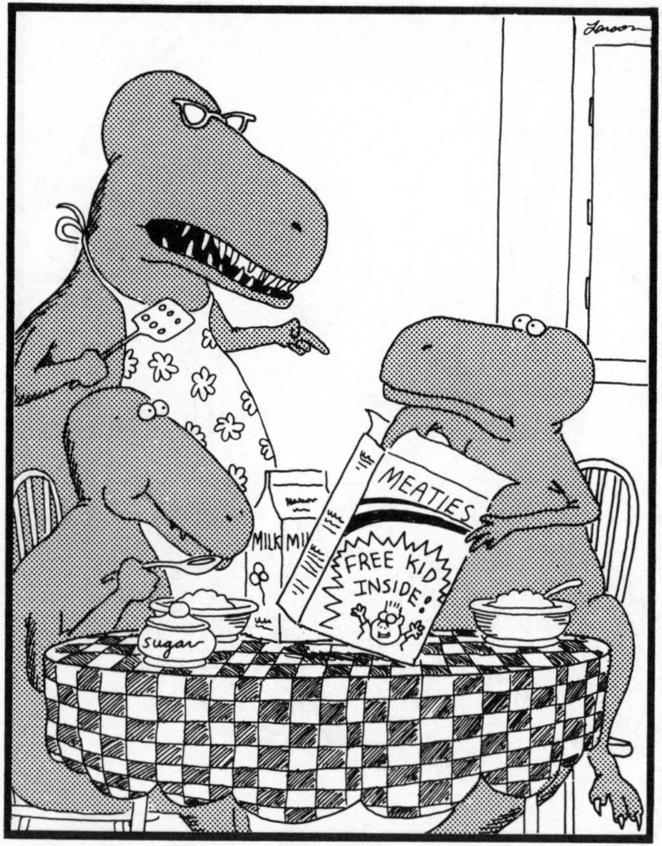
MEATIES
FREE KID INSIDE!
MILK
sugar

"Randy! Just sit down, eat your cereal, and look for that thing later!"

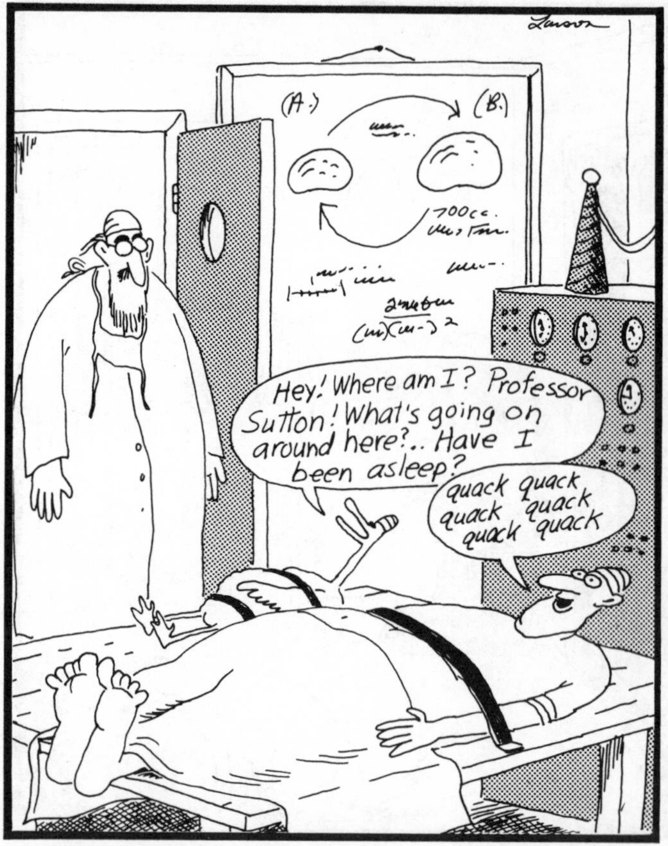
(A.)
(B.)
700cc.
Hey! Where am I? Professor Sutton! What's going on around here?.. Have I been asleep?
quack quack quack quack quack quack

The operation was a success: Later, the duck, with his new human brain, went on to become the leader of a great flock. Irwin, however, was ostracized by his friends and family and eventually just wandered south.

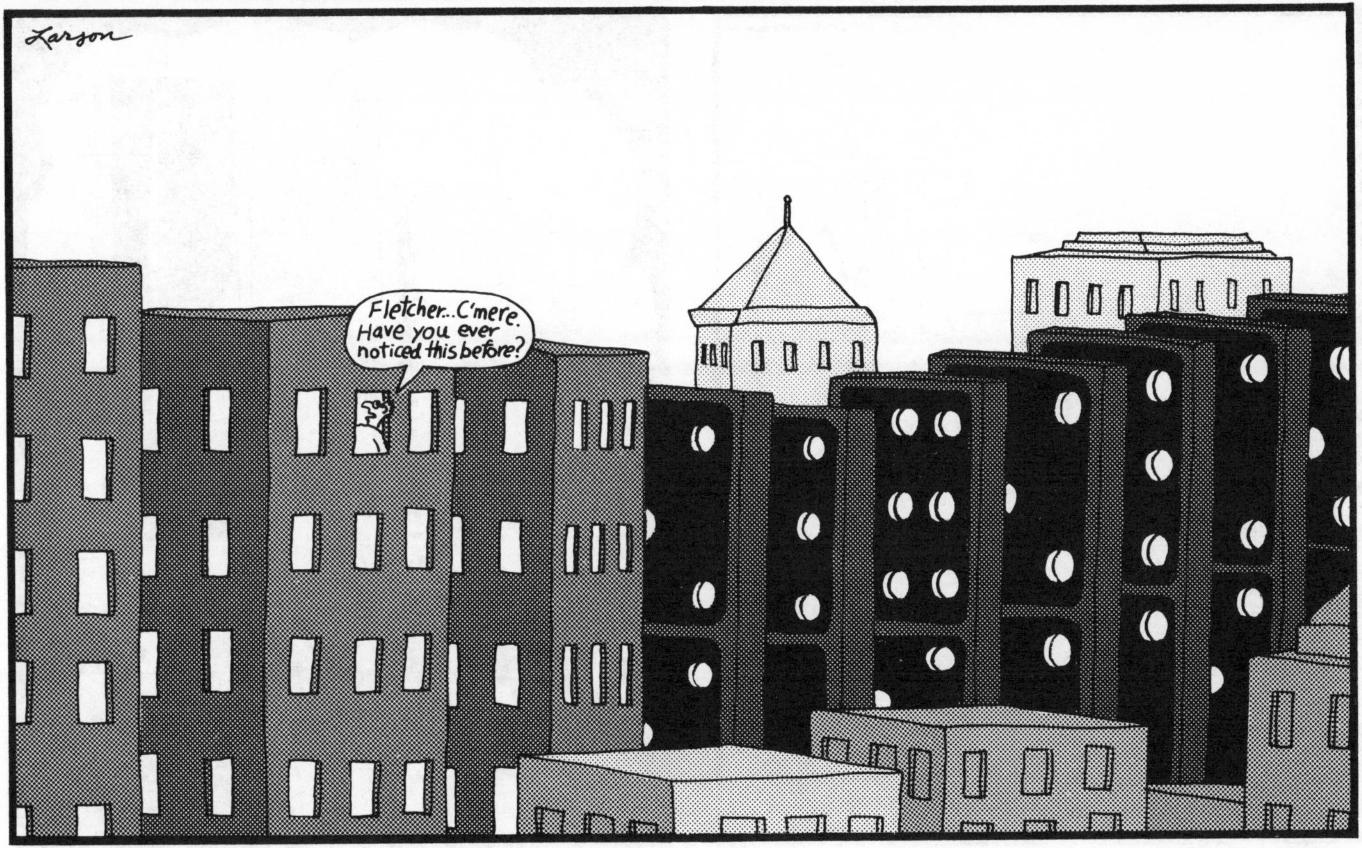
Larson
Fletcher...C'mere. Have you ever noticed this before?

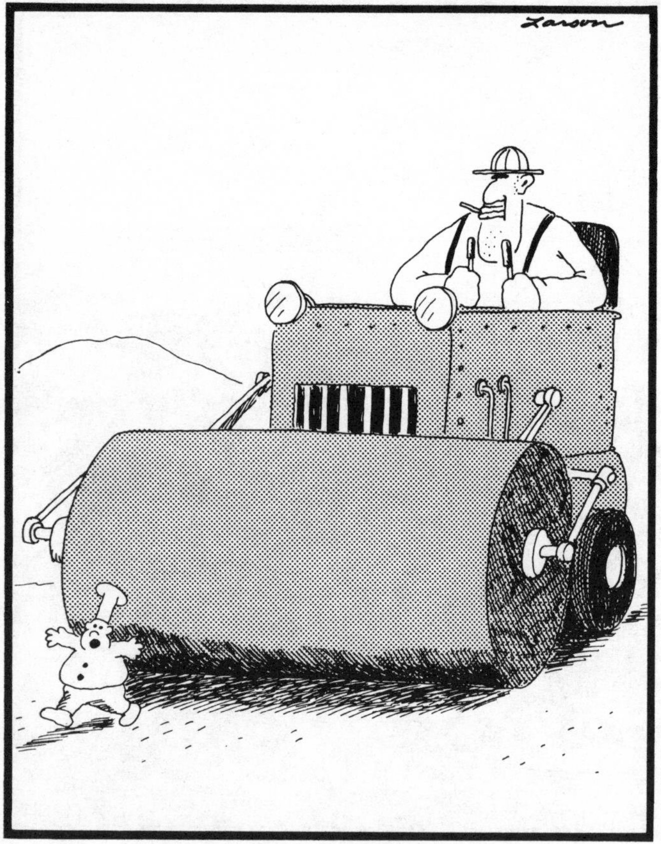
Larson

The Pillsbury Doughboy meets Frank's Asphalt and Concrete Paving Service.

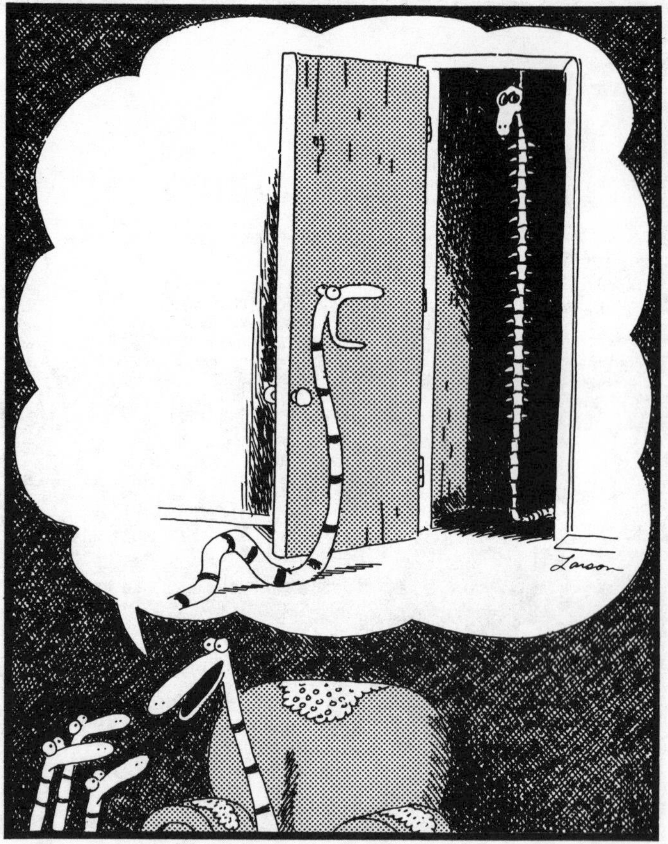
Larson

Snake horror stories

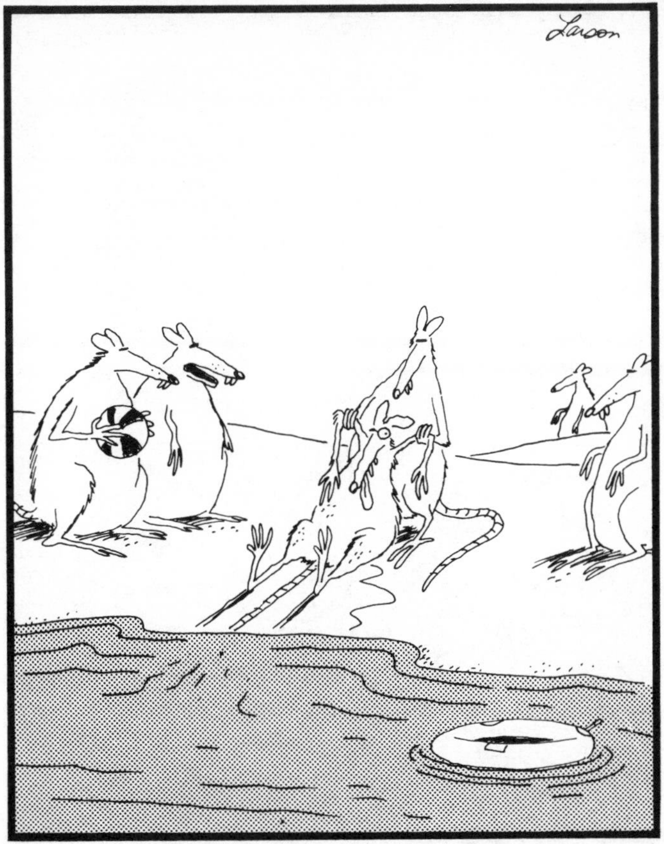
Larson

"Boy, he even looks like a drowned rat."

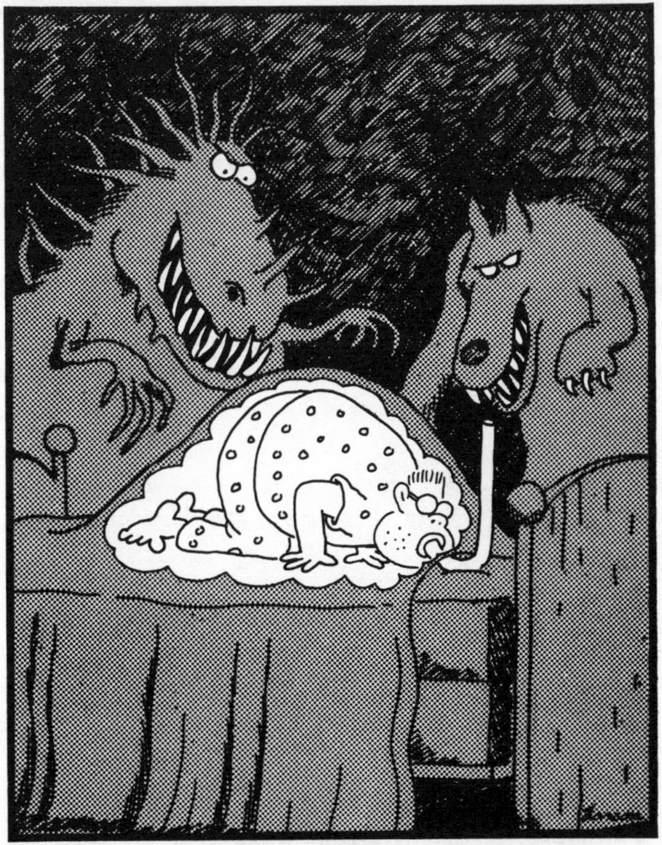

The monster snorkel: Allows your child to breathe comfortably without exposing vulnerable parts to an attack.

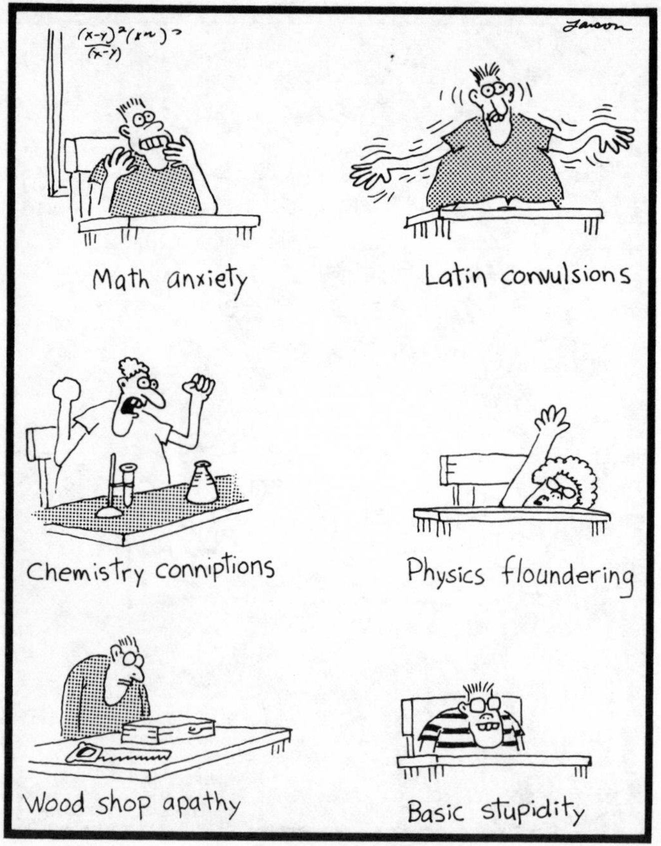
Larson
Math anxiety
Latin convulsions
Chemistry conniptions
Physics floundering
Wood shop apathy
Basic stupidity

Classroom afflictions

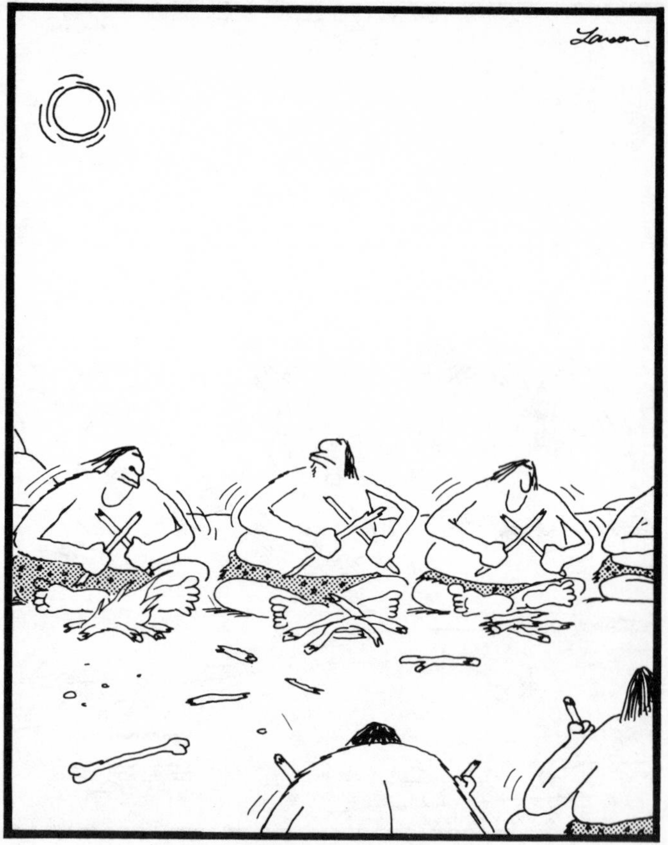
Larson

Early clock-watchers

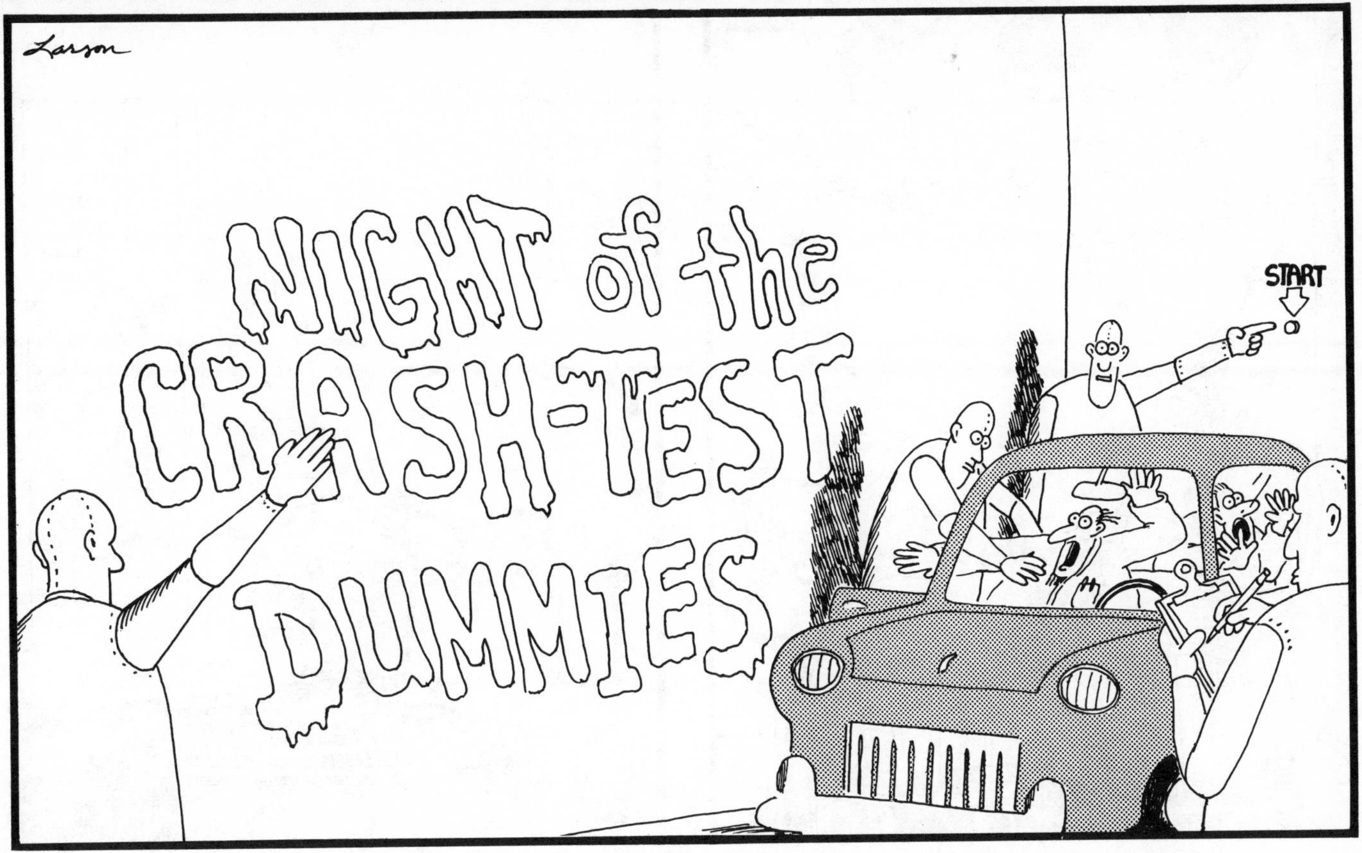
Larson
NIGHT of the CRASH-TEST DUMMIES
START

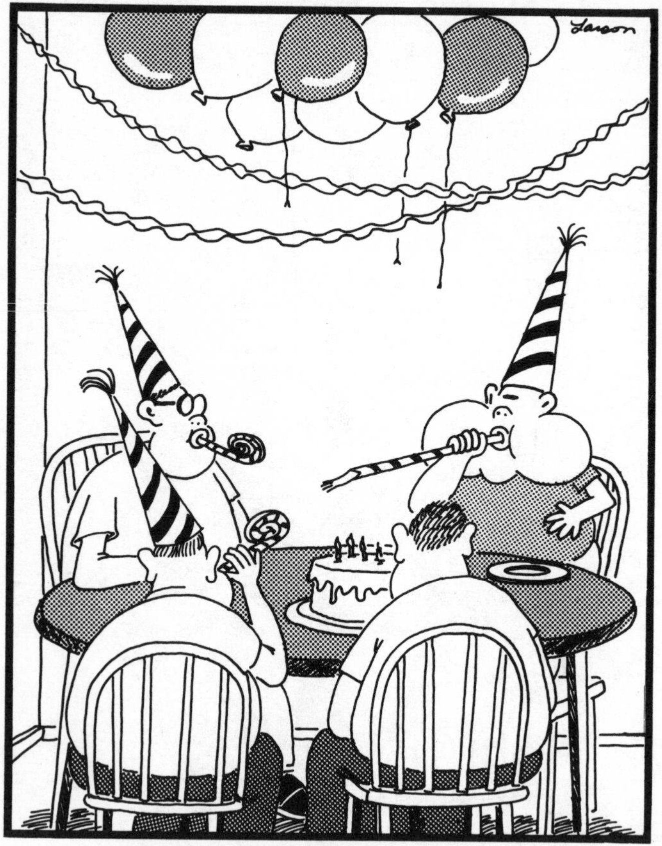
Larson

Dizzy Gillespie's seventh birthday party

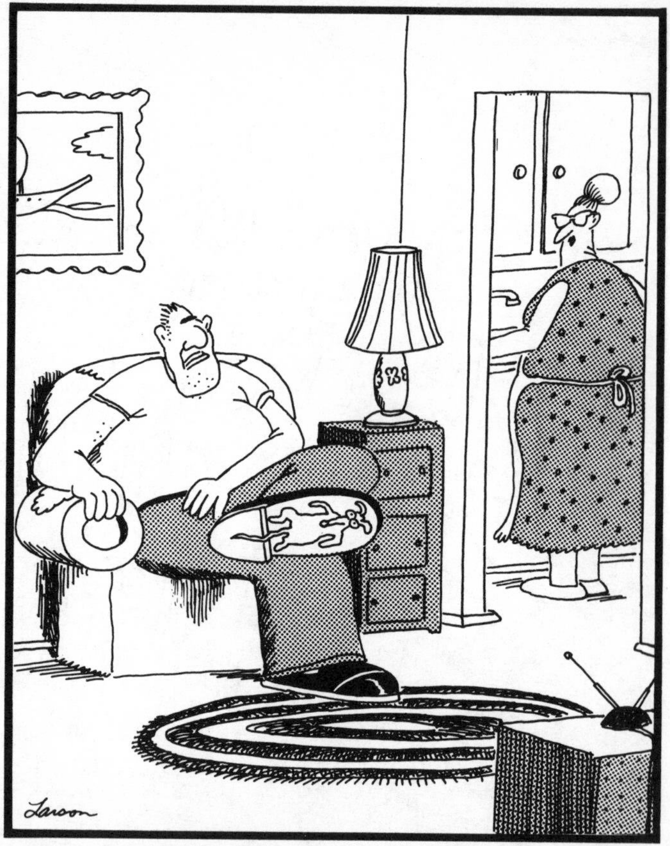
Larson

Helen paused. With an audible "wumph," Muffy's familiar yipping had ended, and only the sounds of Ed's football game now emanated from the living room.

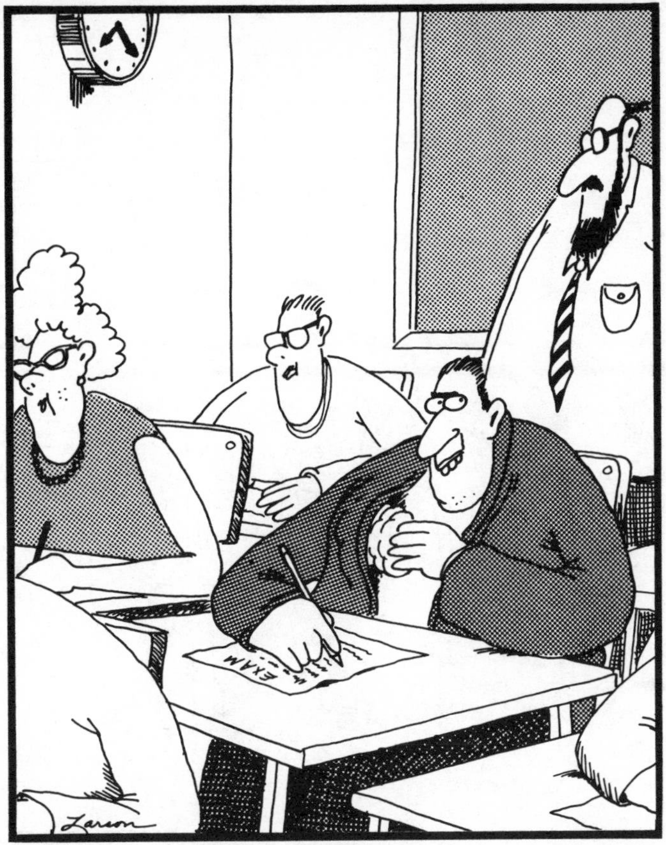
EXAM

Midway through the exam, Allen pulls out a bigger brain.

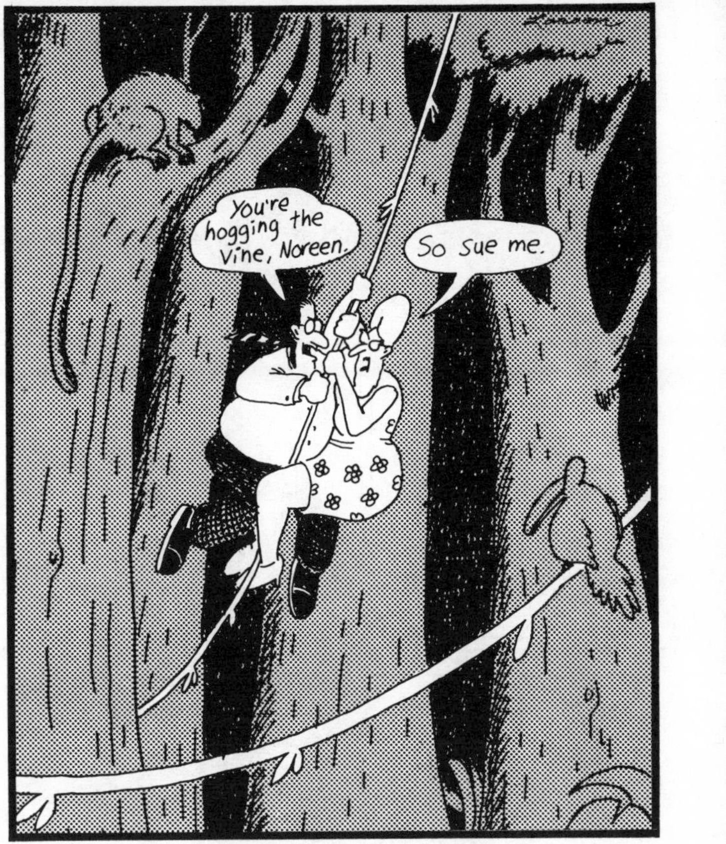
You're hogging the vine, Noreen.
So sue me.

The Hendersons of the jungle

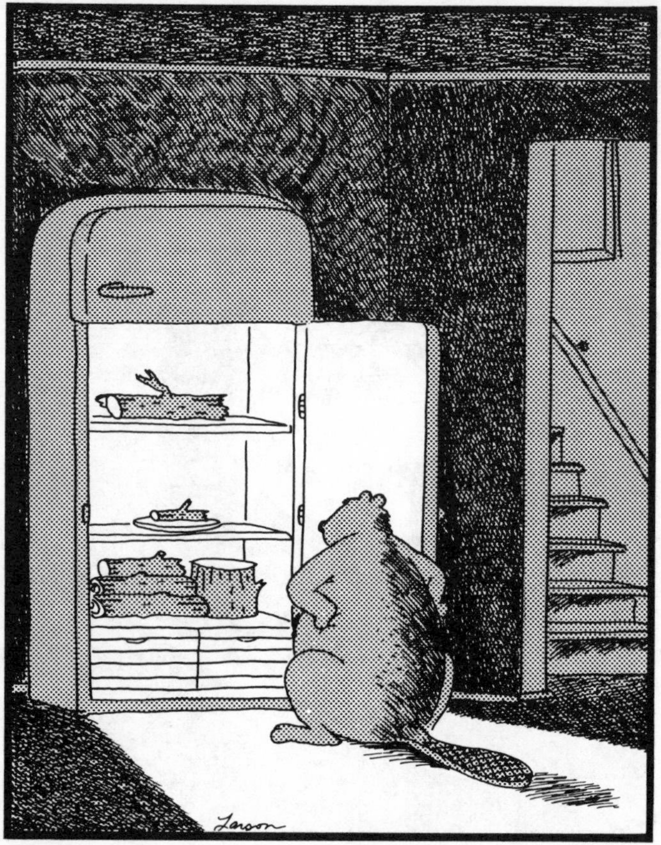
Larson

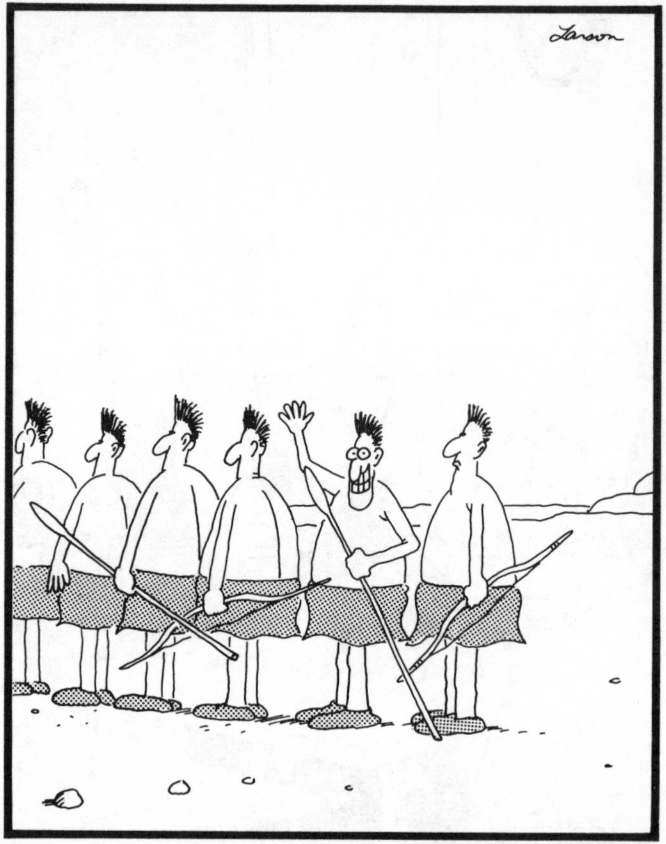
Larson

Second to last of the Mohicans

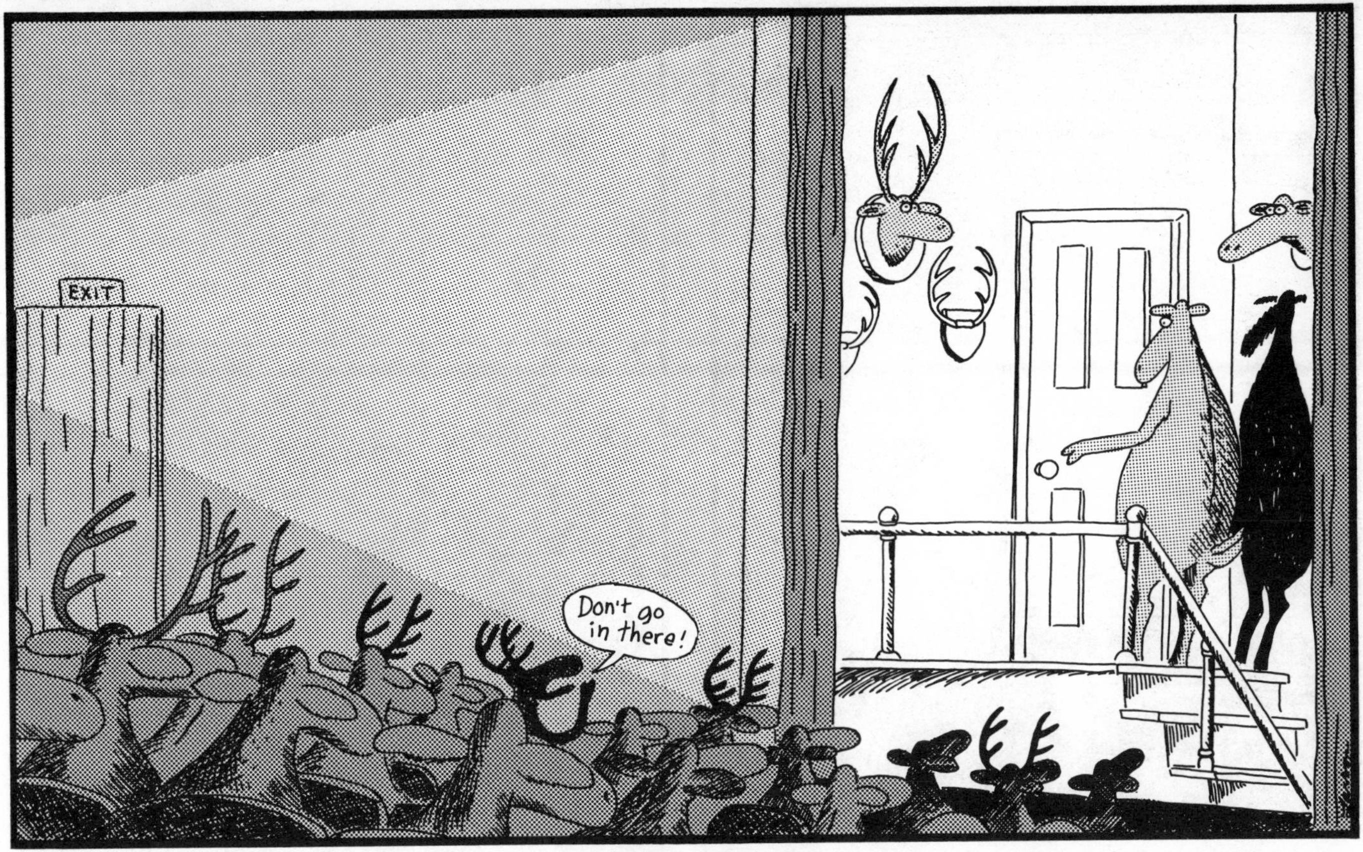
EXIT
Don't go in there!

Horror films of the wild

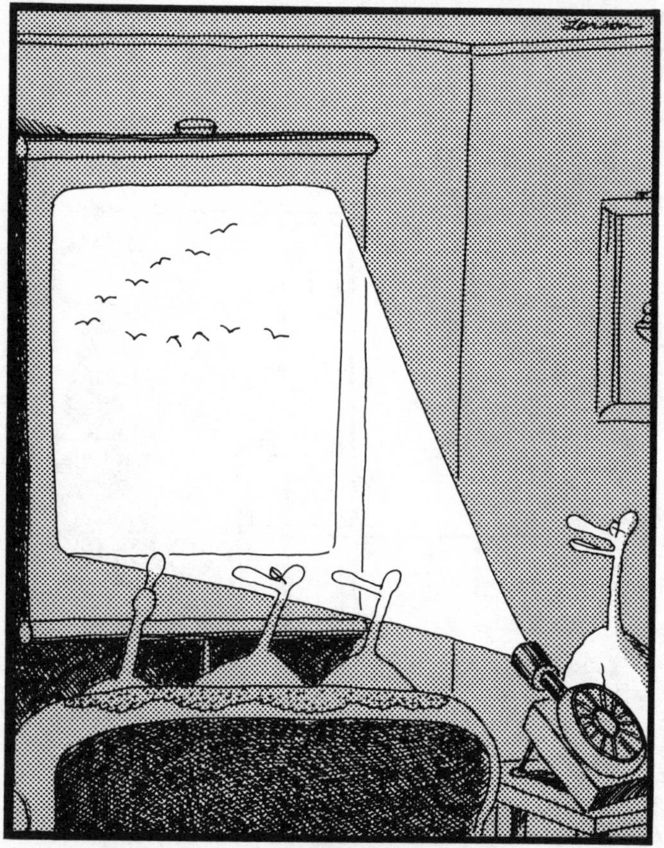
Larson

"And here we are last summer going south. . . . Wait a minute, Irene! We went *north* last summer! The stupid slide's in backward!"

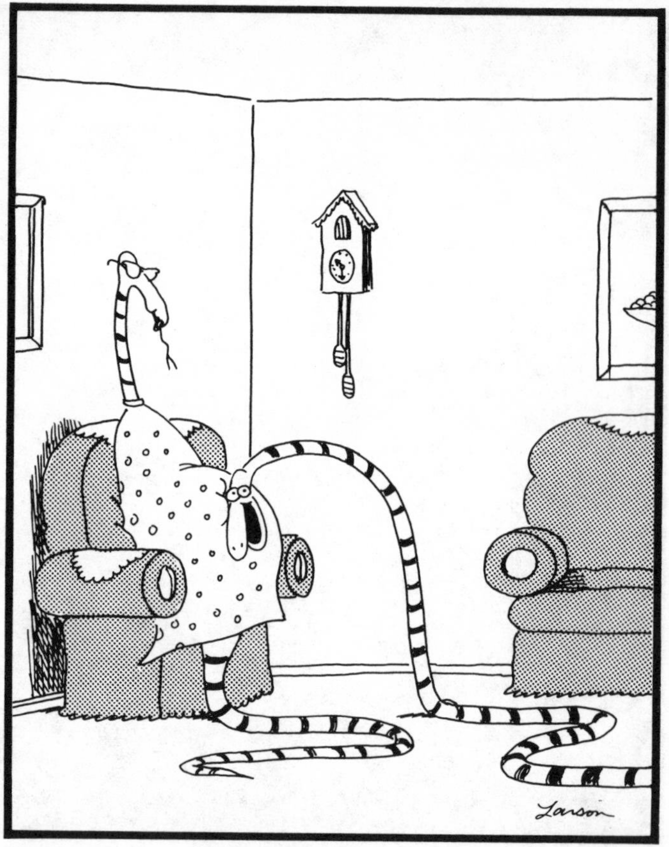
Larson

"I hear 'em! . . . Gee, there must be a *hundred* of the little guys squirmin' around in there!"

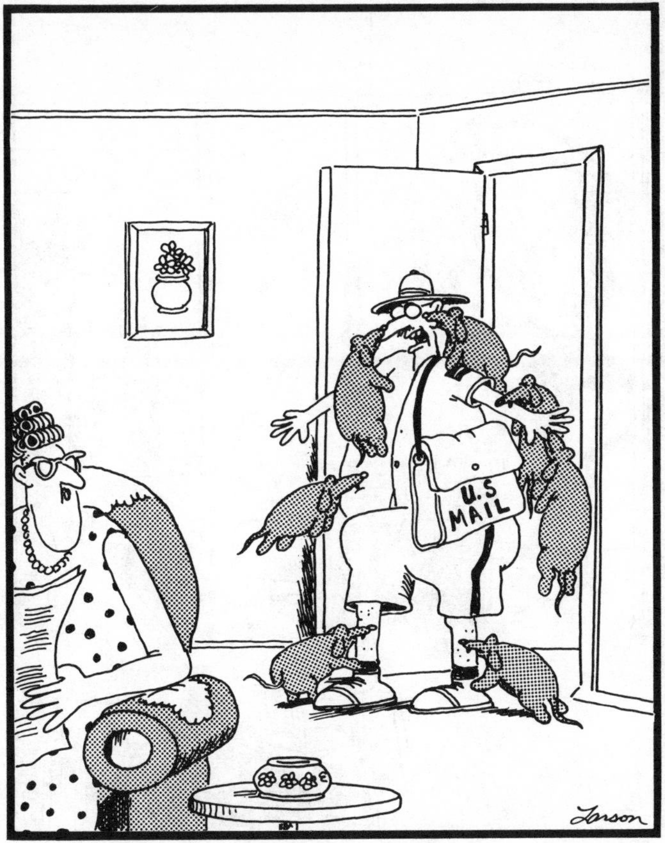
U.S
MAIL
Larson

"Give me a hand here, Etta . . . I got into a nest of wiener dogs over on Fifth and Maple."

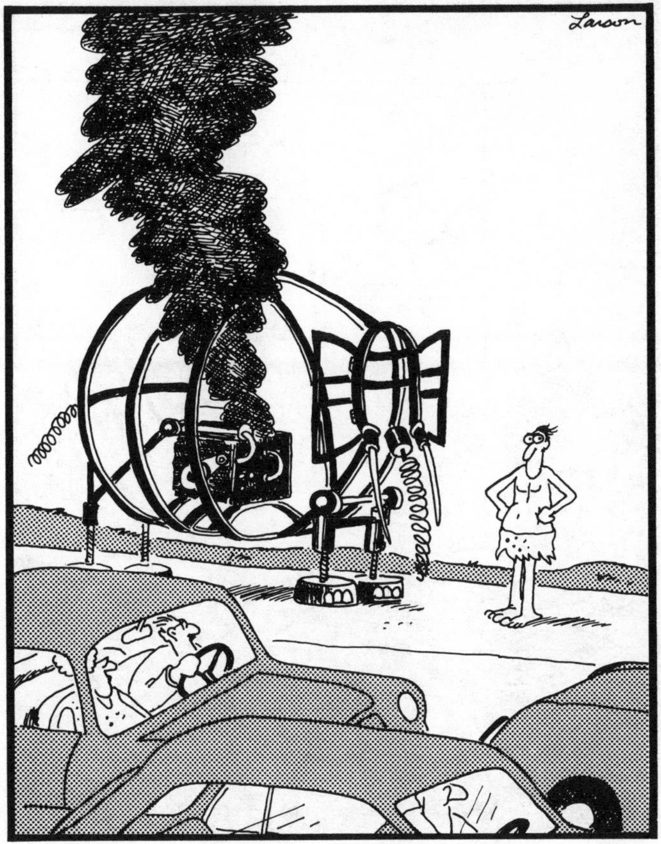
Larson

Tantor burns up on I-90.

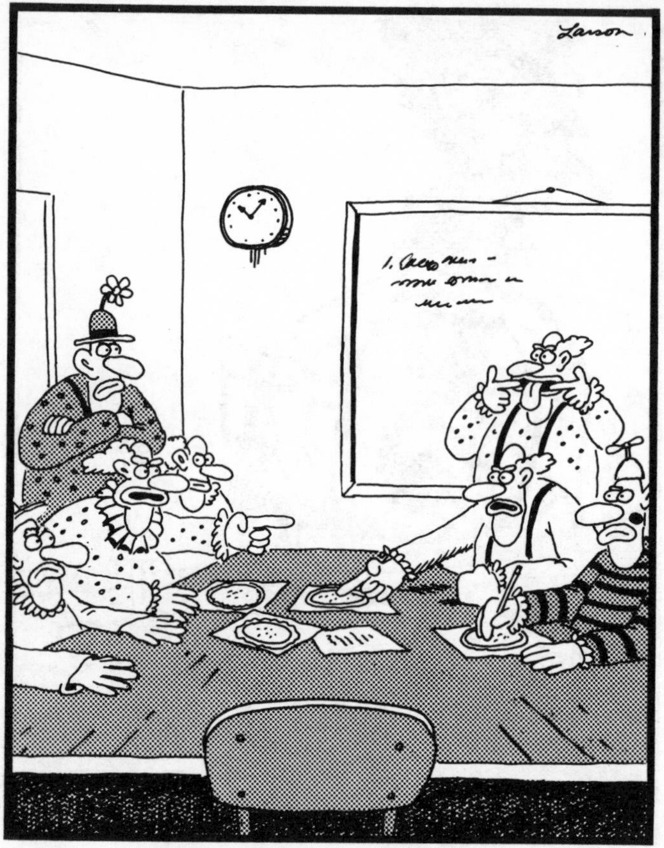
Larson

At the Strategic Pie Limitation Talks

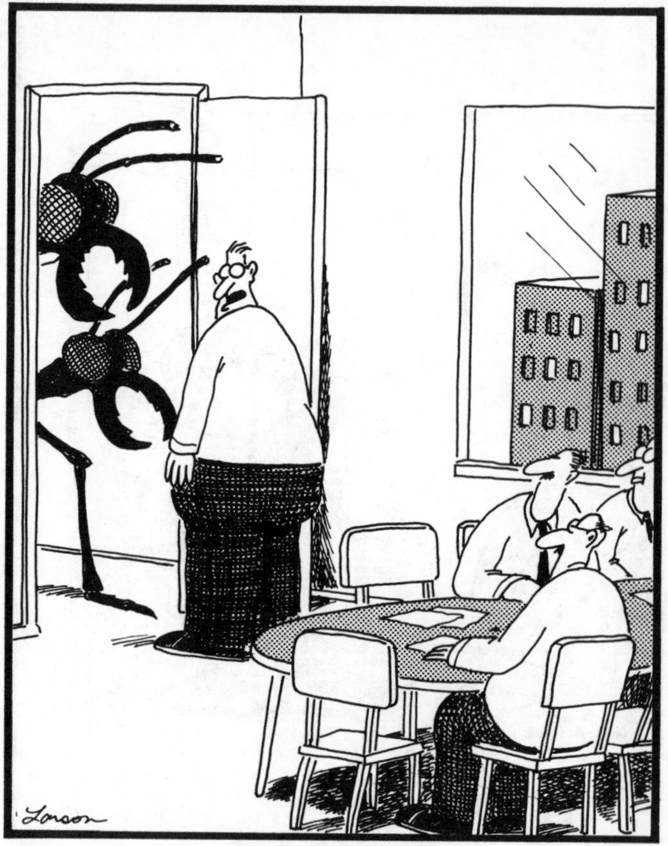
Larson

"It's 'Them,' gentlemen."

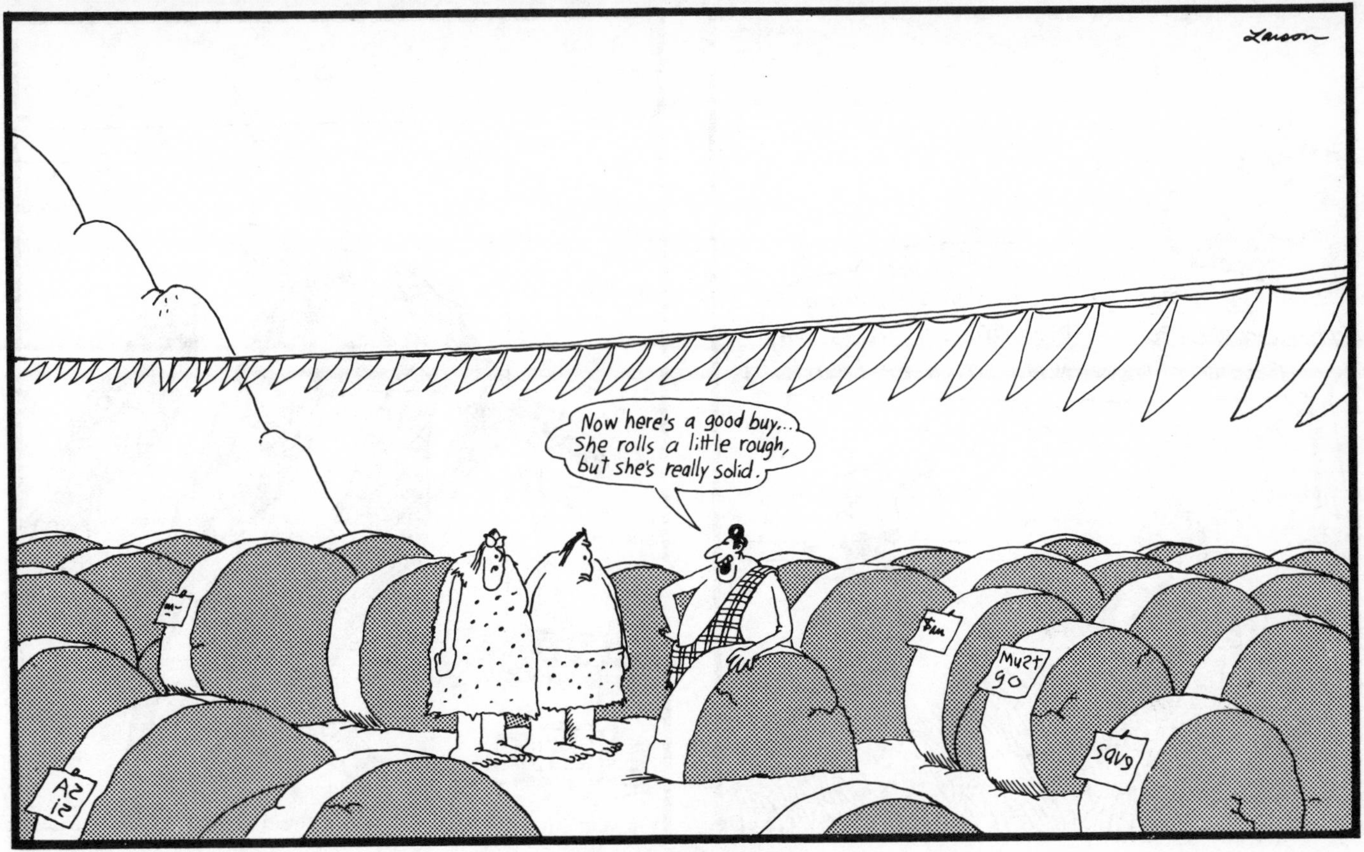
Larson
Now here's a good buy... She rolls a little rough, but she's really solid.
Must go

Early wheeler-dealers

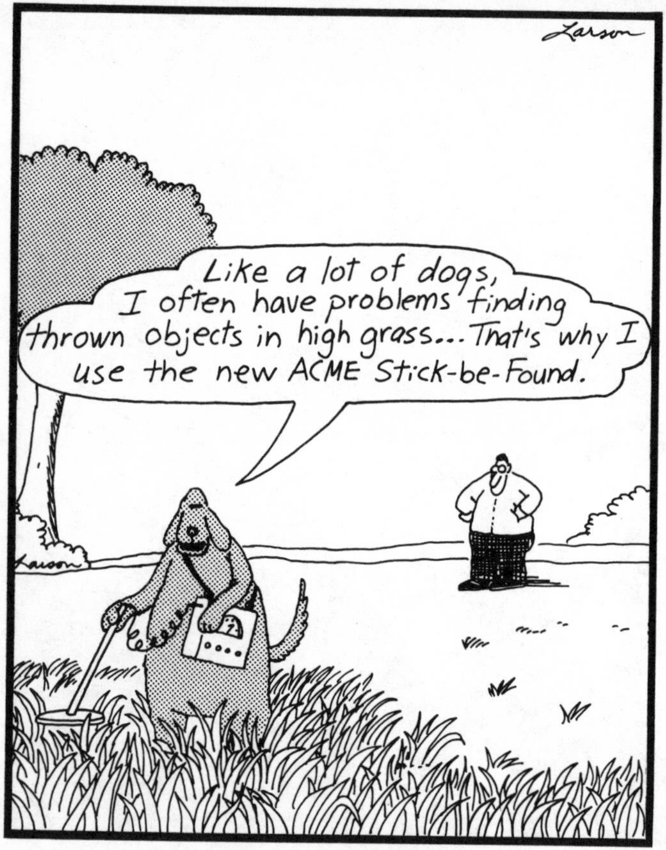
Larson
Like a lot of dogs, I often have problems finding thrown objects in high grass... That's why I use the new ACME Stick-be-Found.
Larson

Dog endorsements

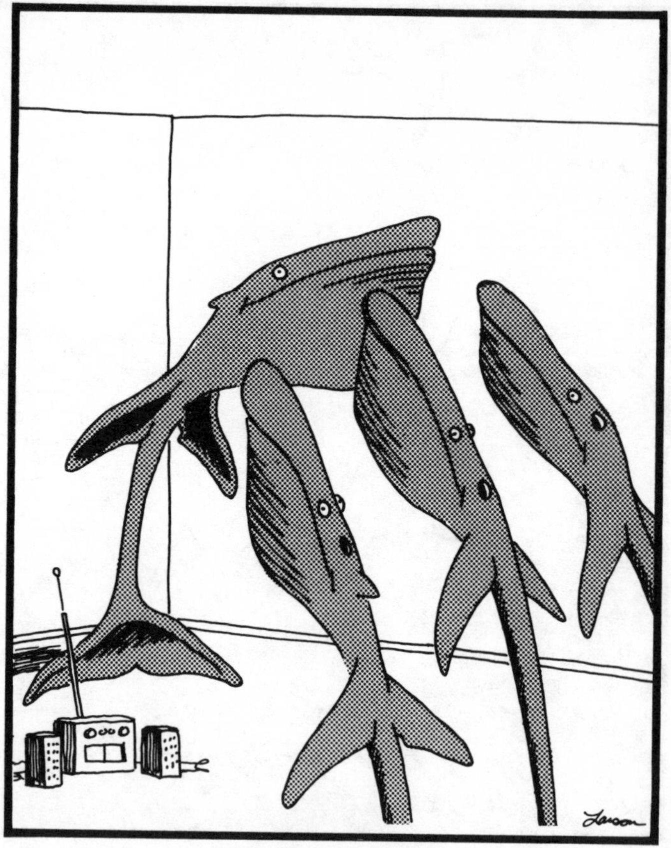
Larson

Whale fitness classes

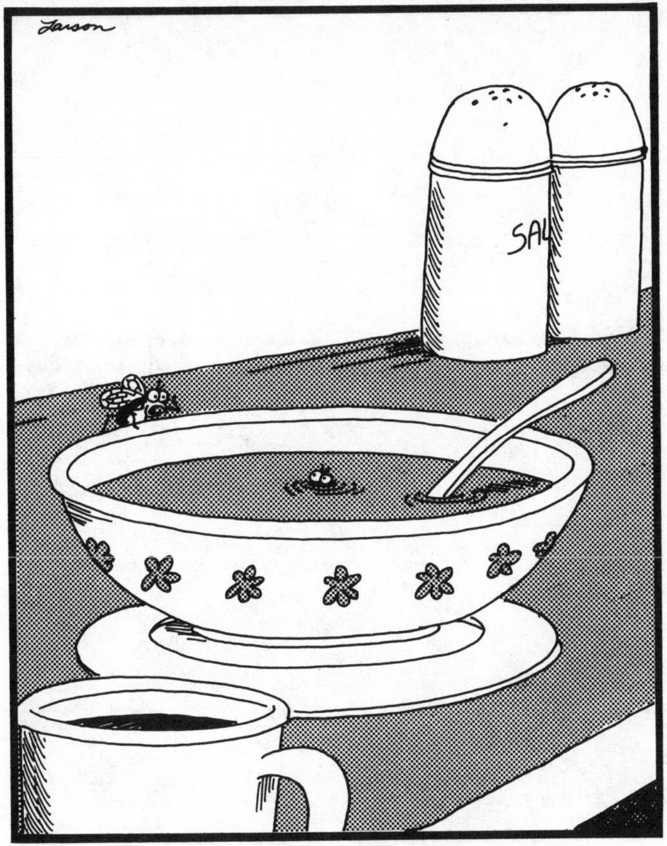
Larson
SAL

"Barbara! I'm goin' for help — tread soup!"

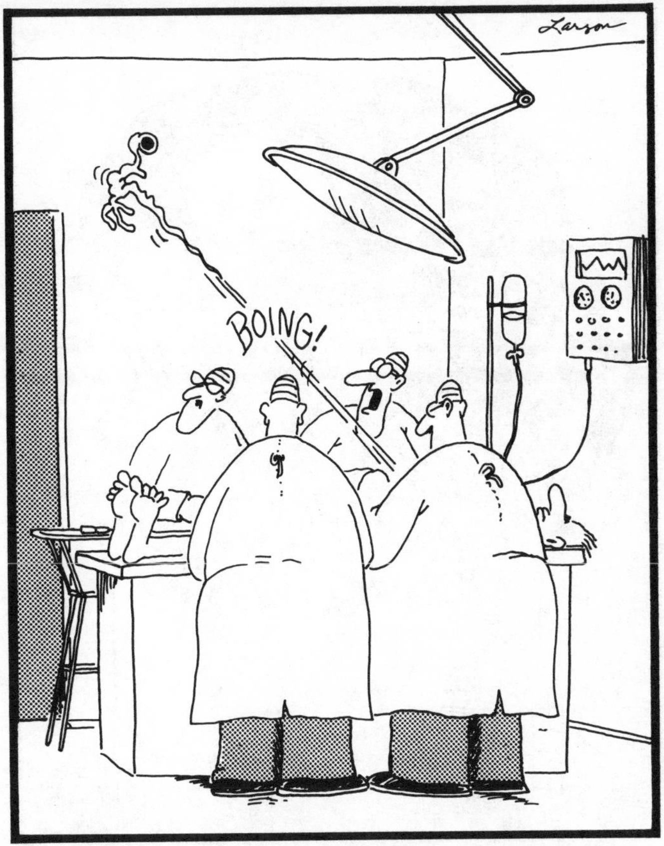
Larson
BOING!

"Whoa! Watch where that thing lands — we'll probably need it."

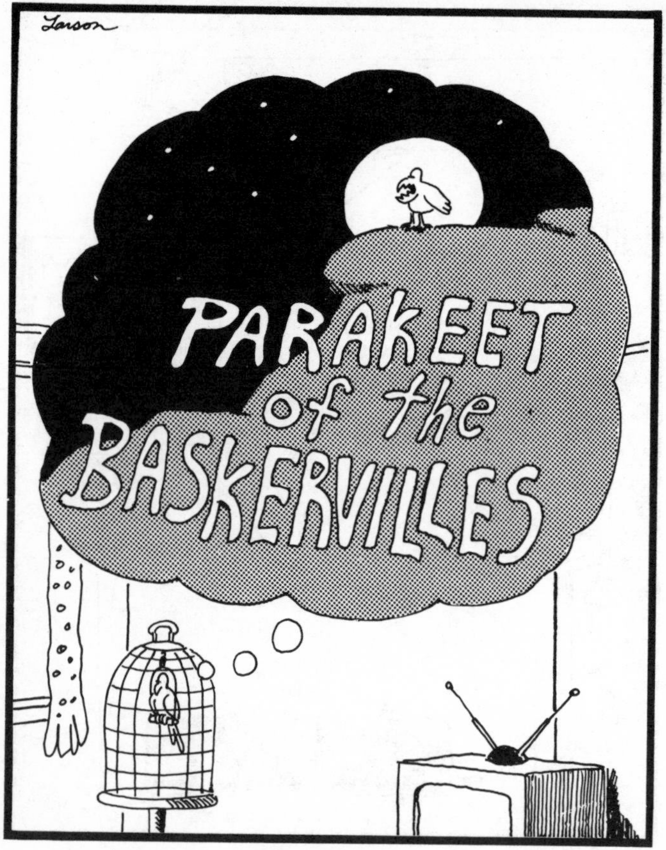
Larson
PARAKEET of the BASKERVILLES

Buddy's dreams

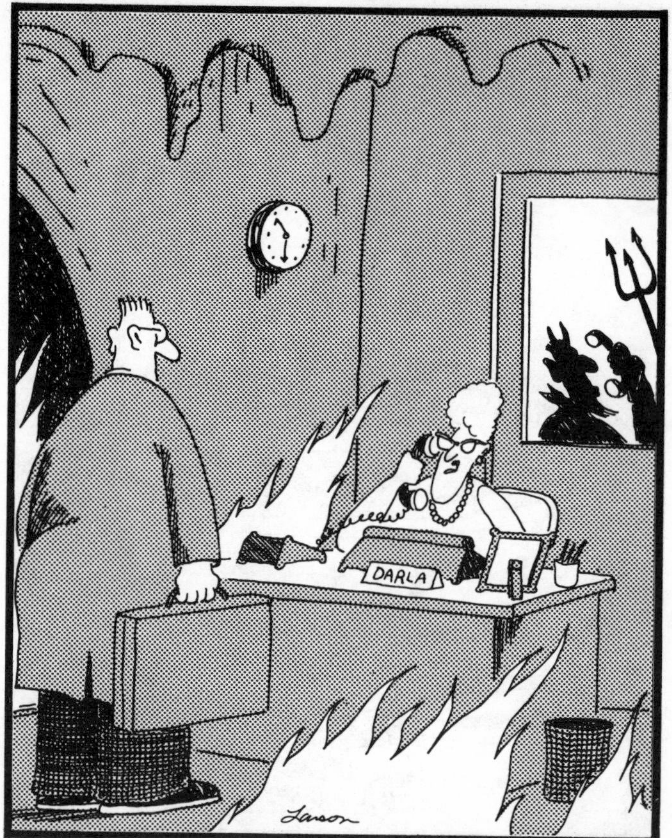
DARLA
Larson

"Sorry to bother you, sir, but there's another salesman out here — you want me to tell him to go to heaven?"

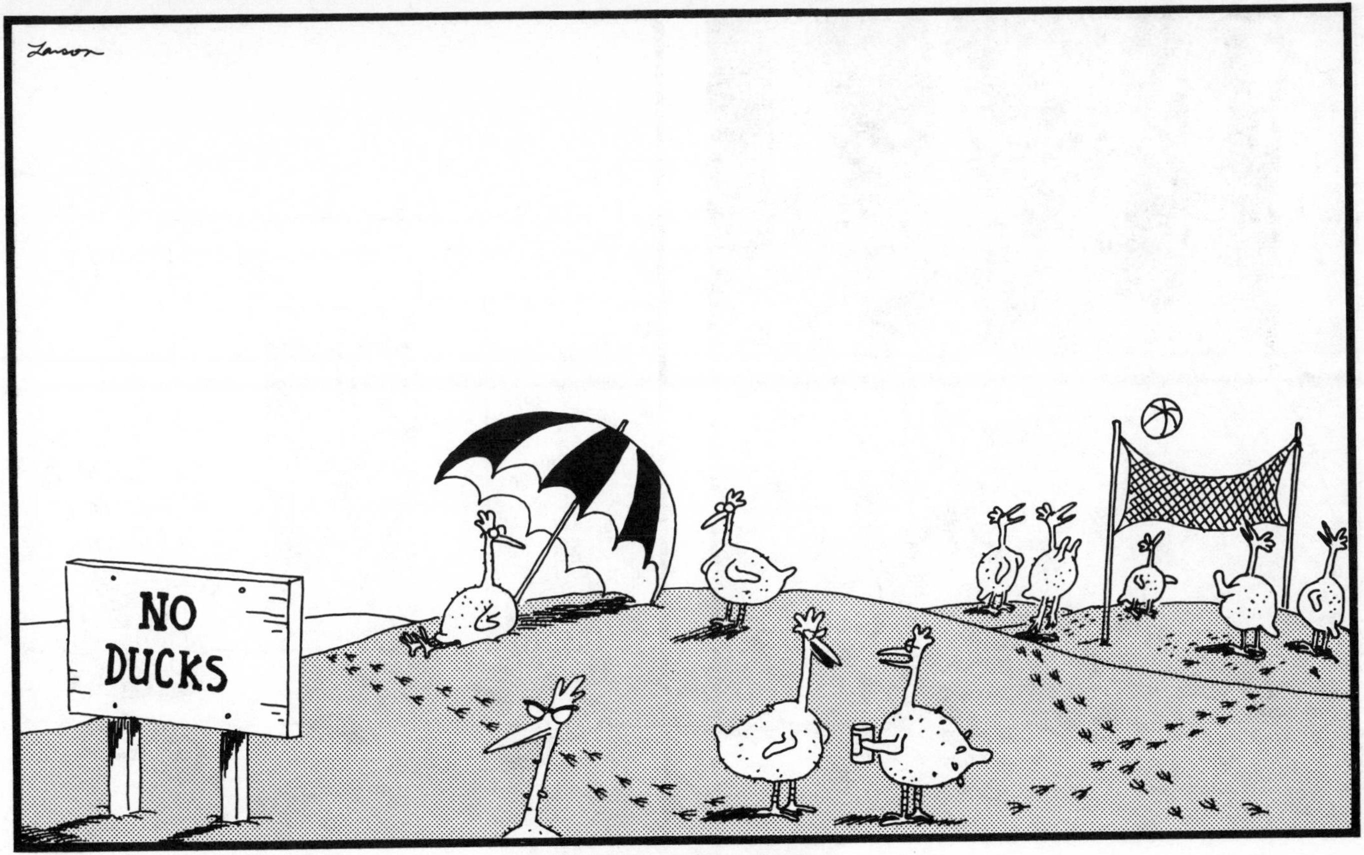
Larson
NO DUCKS
Chicken nudist colonies

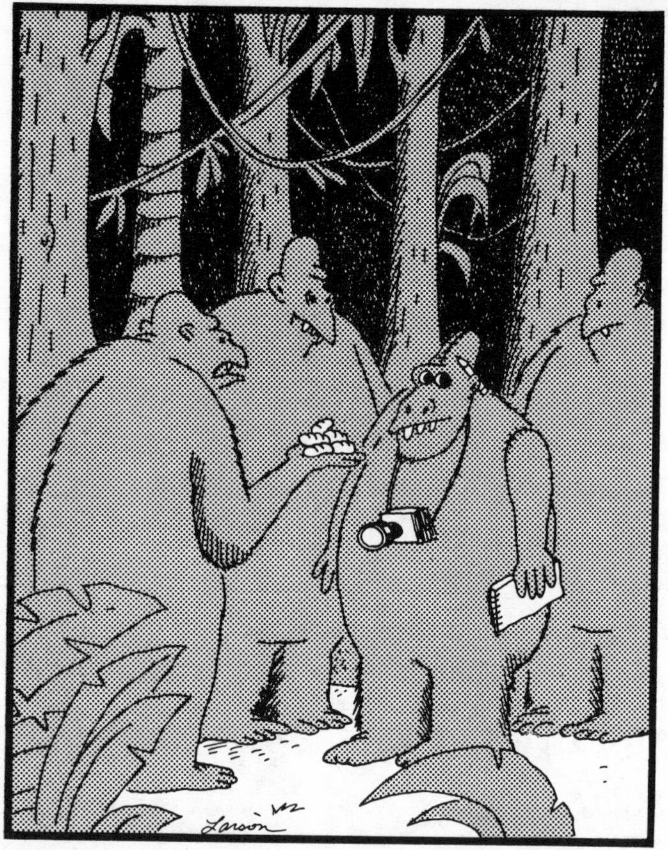
Larson

"So, you're a *real* gorilla, are you? Well, guess you wouldn't mind munchin' down a few beetle grubs, would you? . . . In fact, we wanna see you chug 'em!"

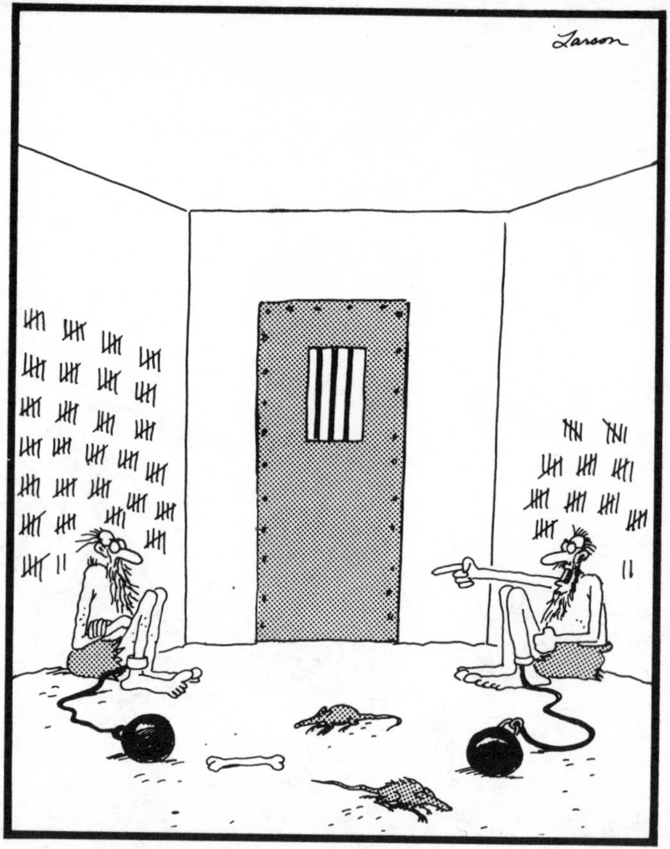
Larson

"And another thing! I'm sick and tired of you callin' me 'new kid' all the time!"

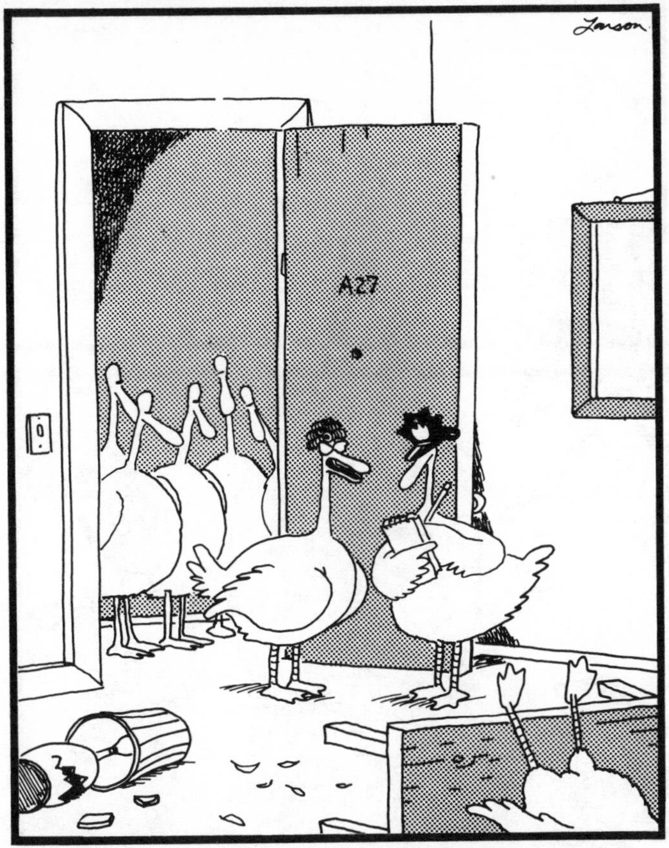
Larson
A27

"Well, from across the hall I could hear this heated argument, followed by sounds of a scuffle. Suddenly, there was this tremendous, blood-curdling 'quaaaaacck!' That's when I called."

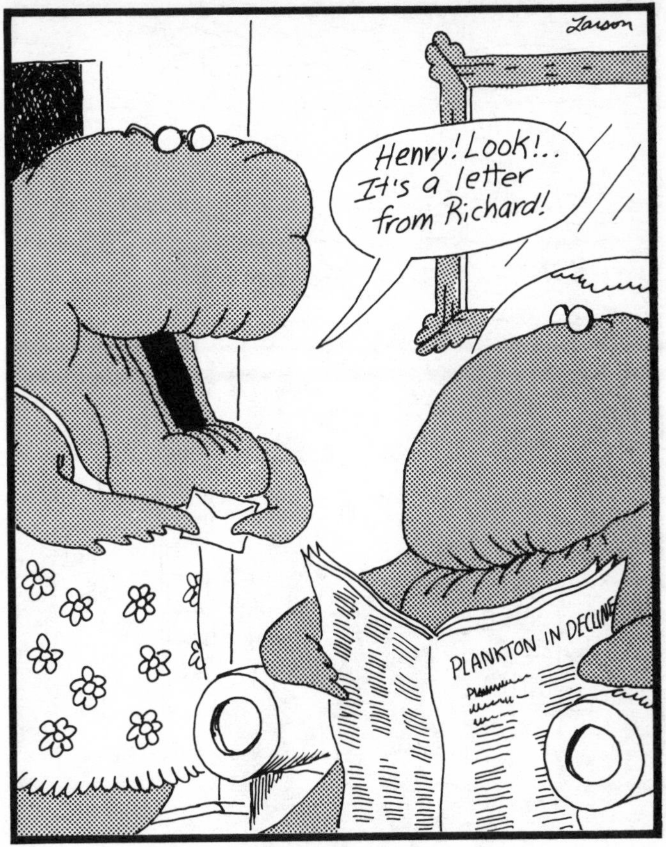
Larson
Henry! Look!.. It's a letter from Richard!
PLANKTON IN DECLINE

Moby's parents

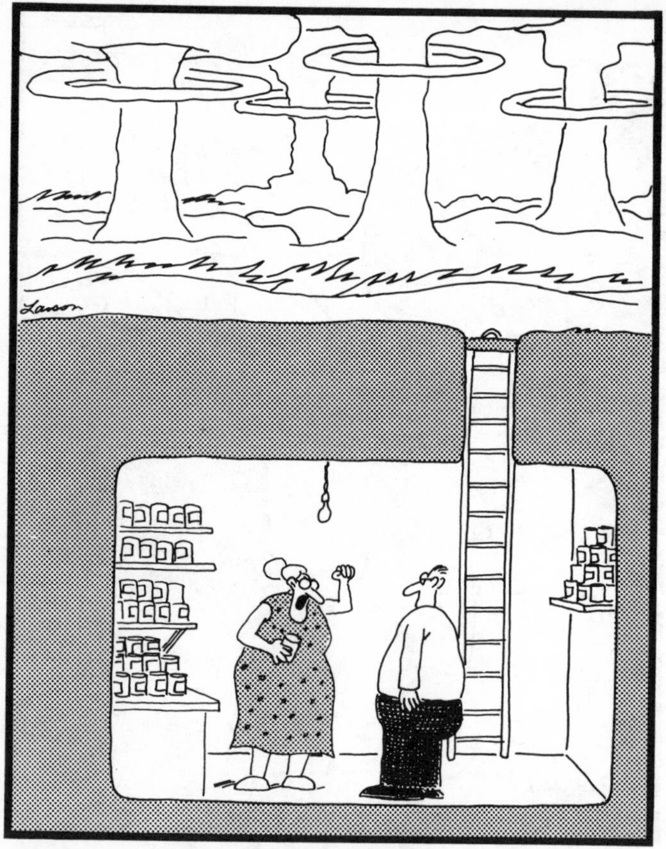
Larson

"How many times did I say it, Harold? How many times? 'Make sure that bomb shelter's got a can opener — ain't much good without a can opener,' I said."

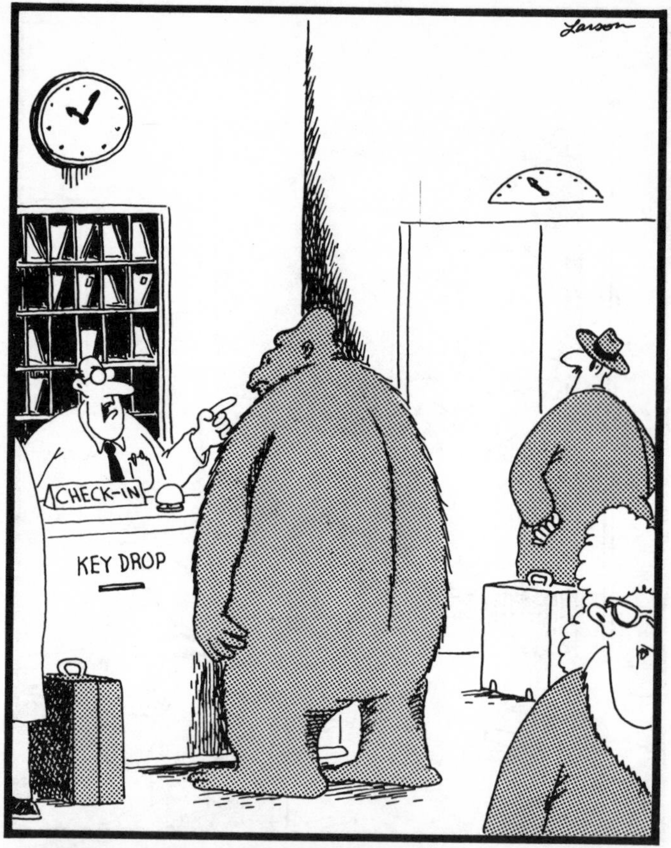
Larson
CHECK-IN
KEY DROP

"Look. I'm sorry . . . If you weighed 500 pounds, we'd certainly accommodate you — but it's simply a fact that a *400*-pound gorilla does *not* sleep anywhere he wants to."

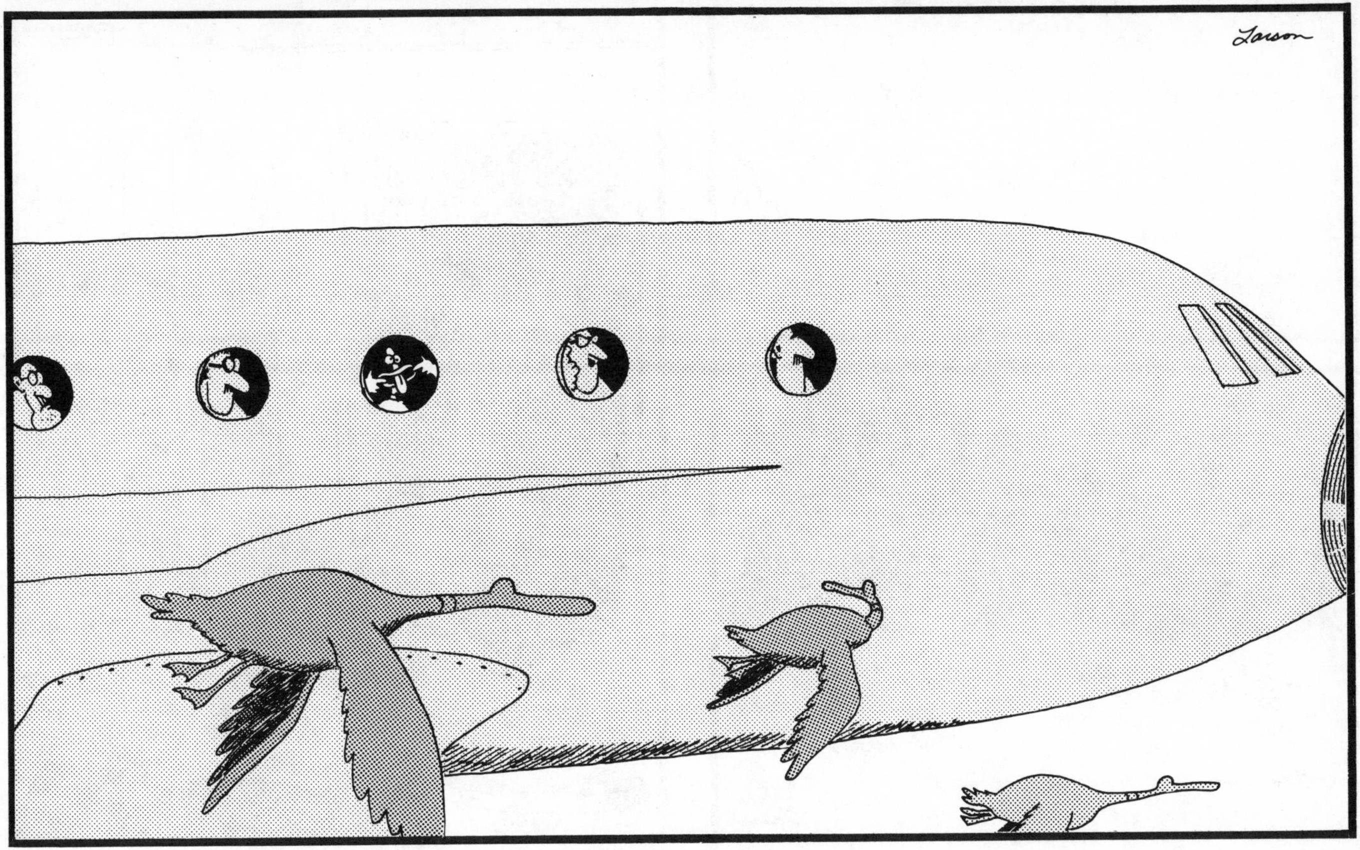
Larson

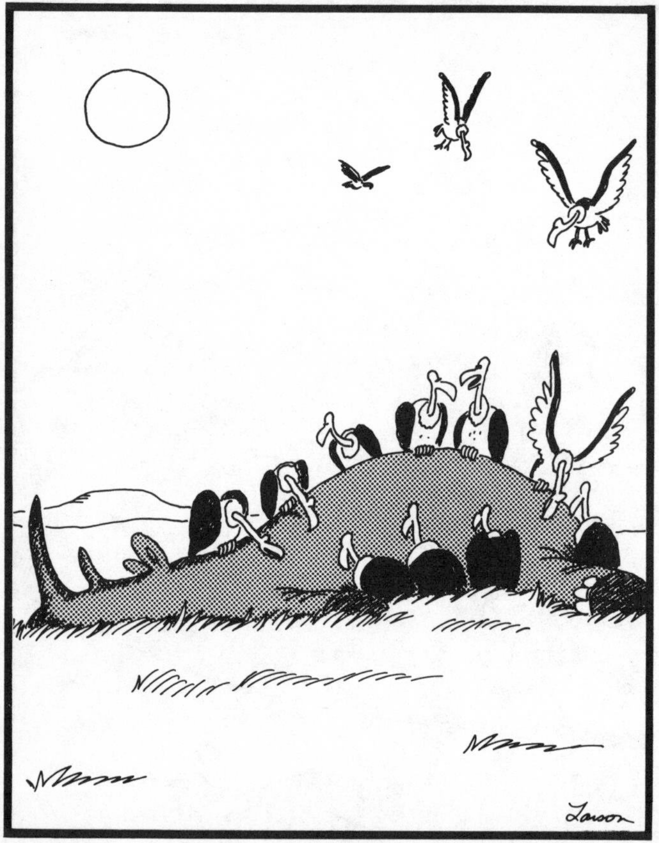
Larson

"Just think . . . Here we are, the afternoon sun beating down on us, a dead, bloated rhino underfoot, and good friends flying in from all over. . . . I tell you, Ed, this is the best of times."

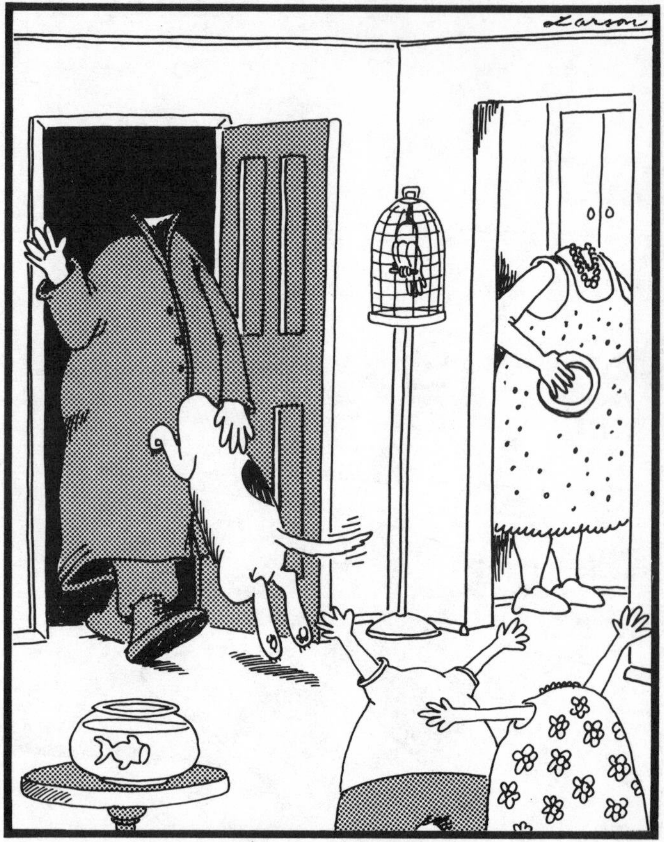
Larson

The Headless Horsefamily

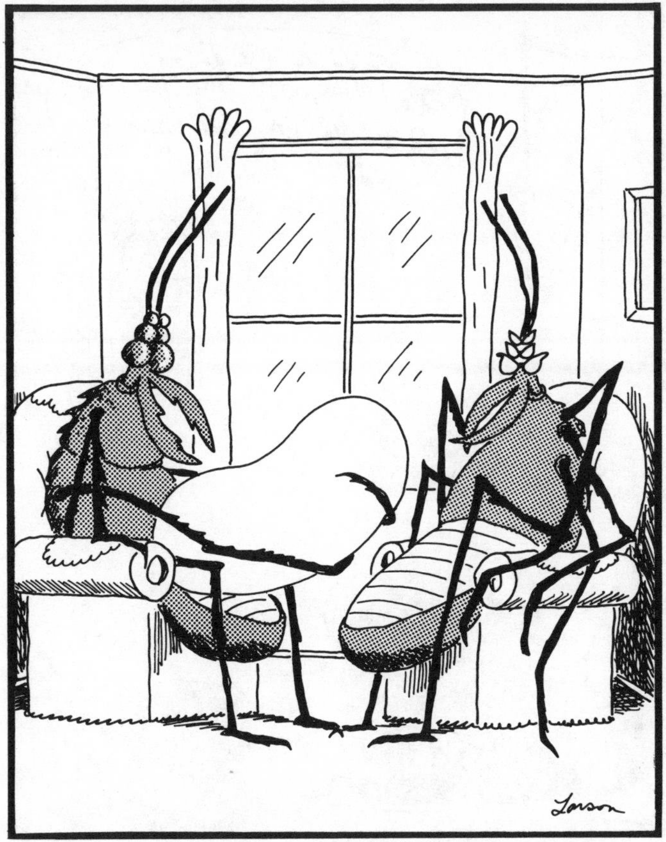
Larson

"Well, Roger's hoping for a male and I'd like a little female. . . . But, really, we'll both be content if it just has six eyes and eight legs."

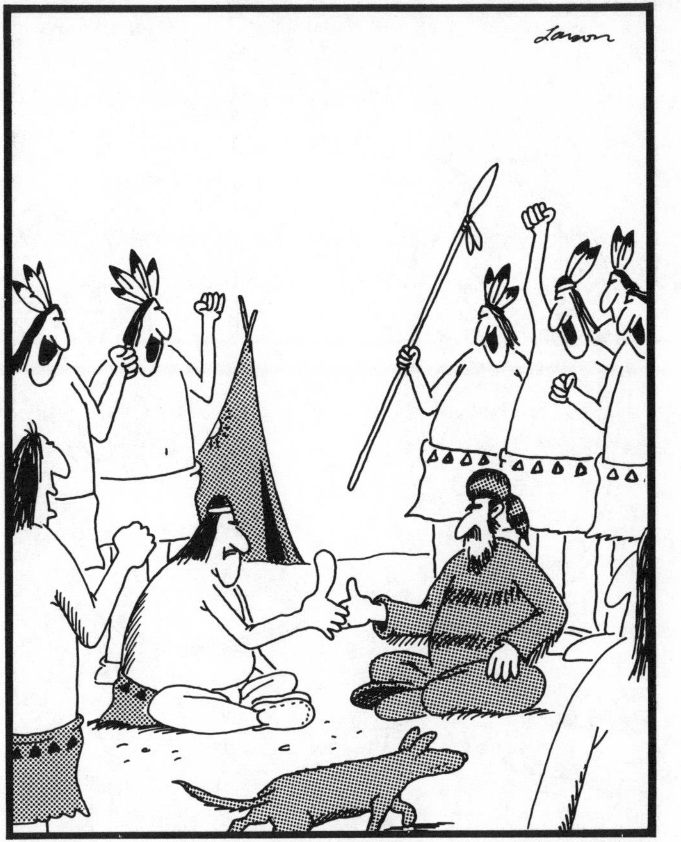
Larson

To win the tribe's respect, Jed first had to defeat their best thumb-wrestler.

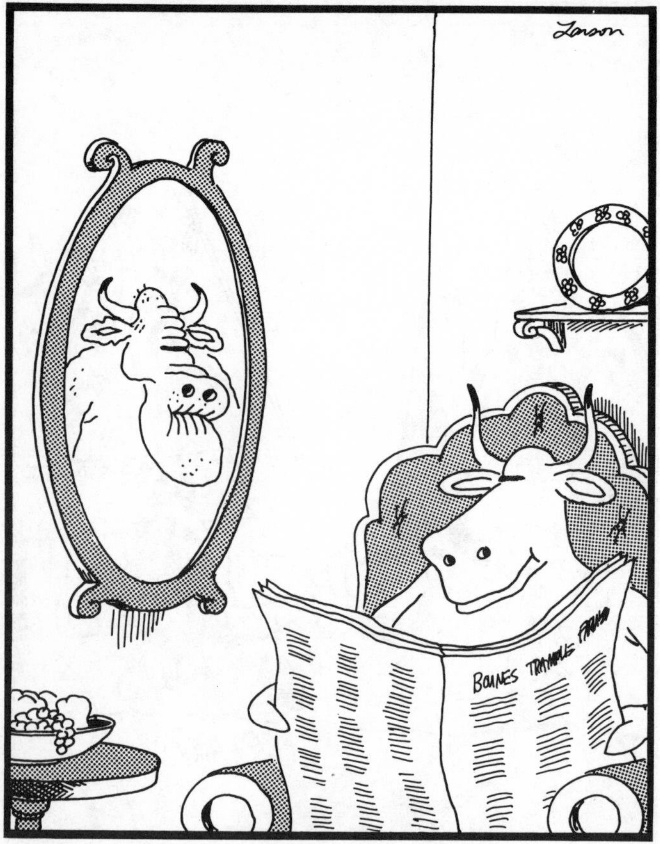
Larson

The portrait of Dorian Cow

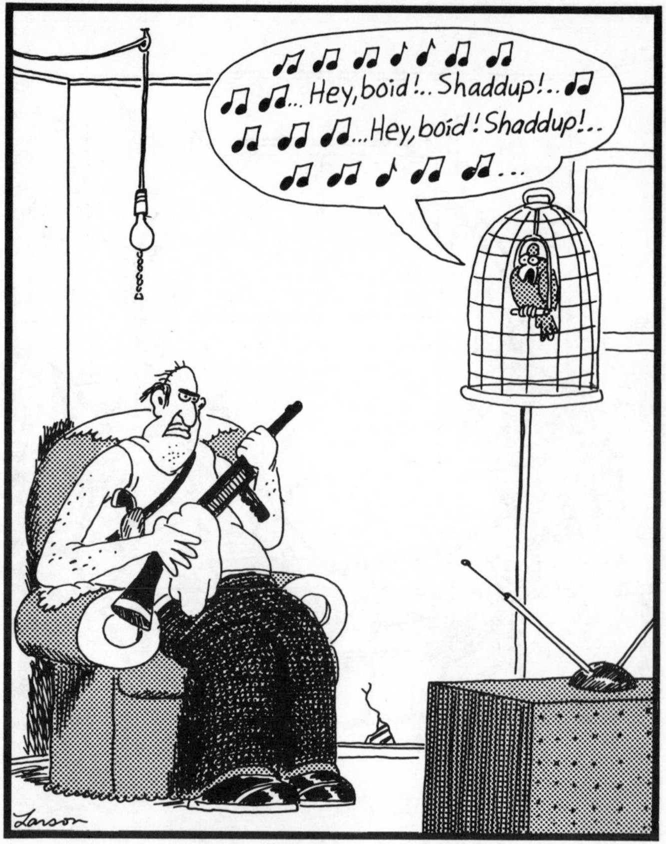
♫ ♫ ♫ ♪ ♪ ♫ ♫
♫ ♫... Hey, boid!.. Shaddup!.. ♫
♫ ♫ ♫...Hey, boid! Shaddup!..
♫ ♫ ♪ ♫ ♫...
Larson

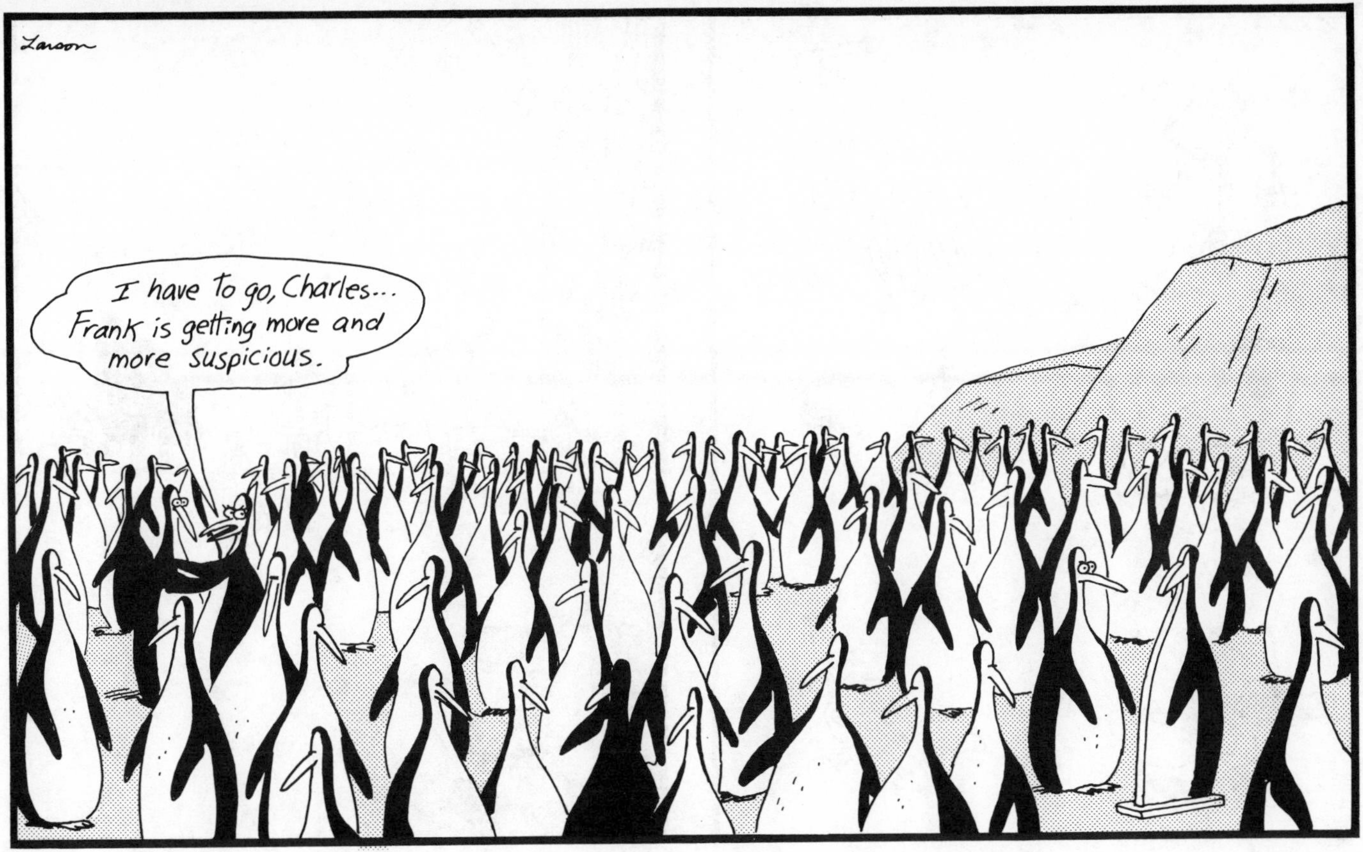
Larson
I have to go, Charles... Frank is getting more and more suspicious.

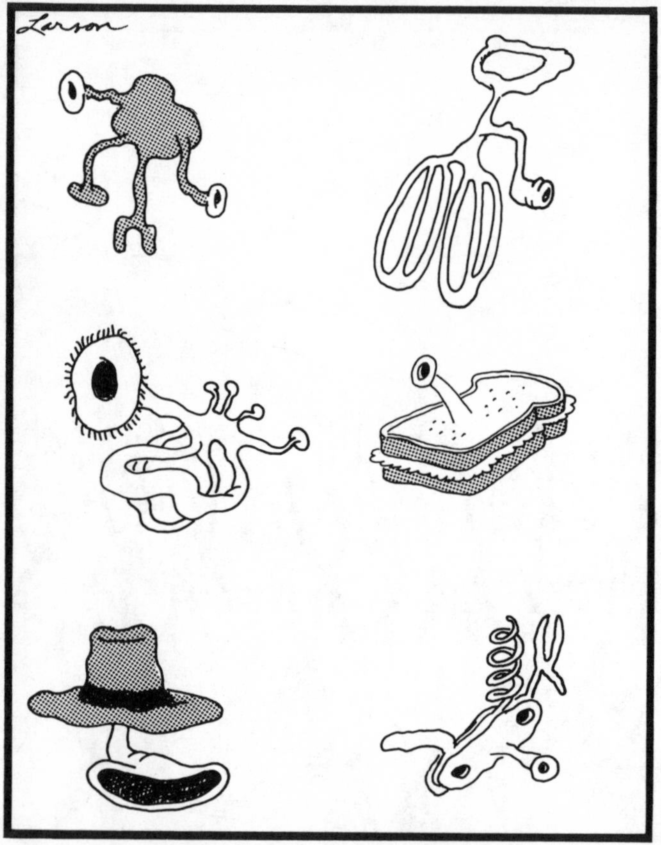
Larson

Some of the non-vital organs

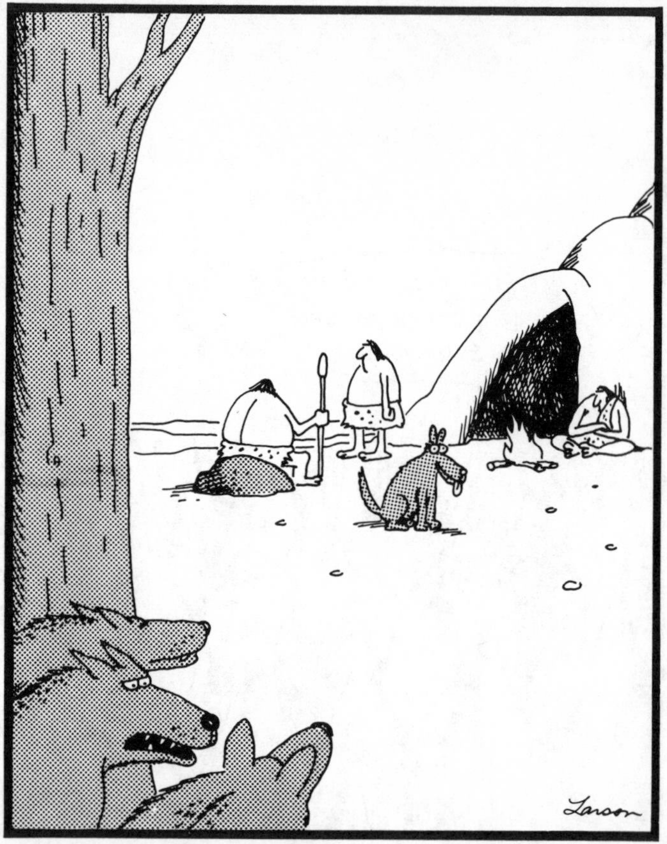
Larson

"It's Bob, all right . . . but look at those vacuous eyes, that stupid grin on his face — he's been domesticated, I tell you."

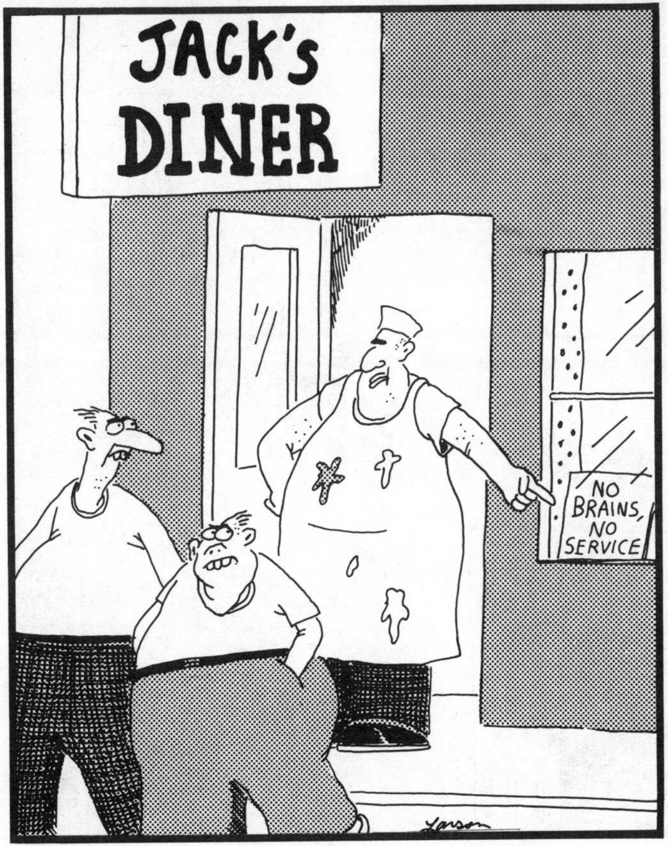
JACK'S DINER
NO BRAINS, NO SERVICE
Larson

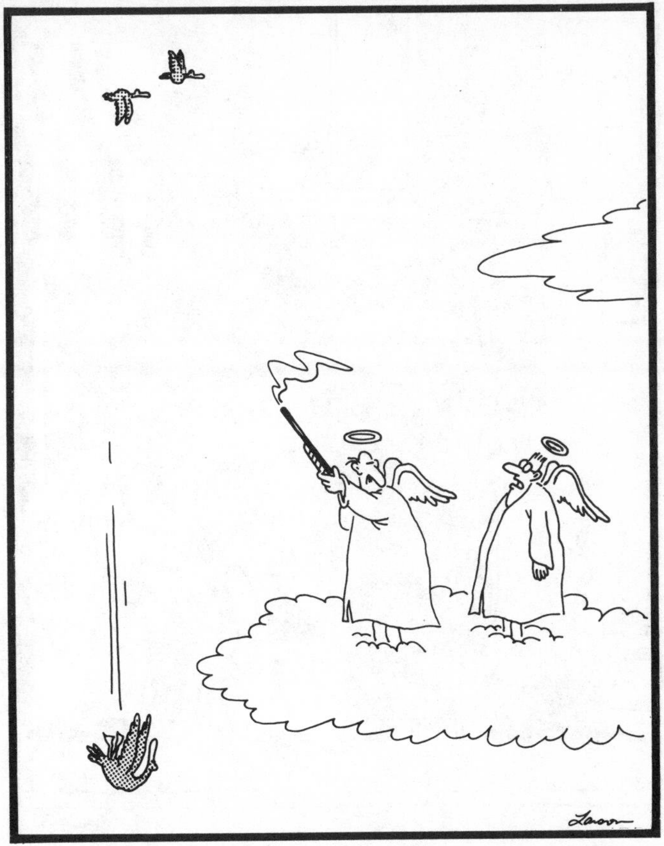
Larson
"You sure you're supposed to be doin' that, Mitch?"

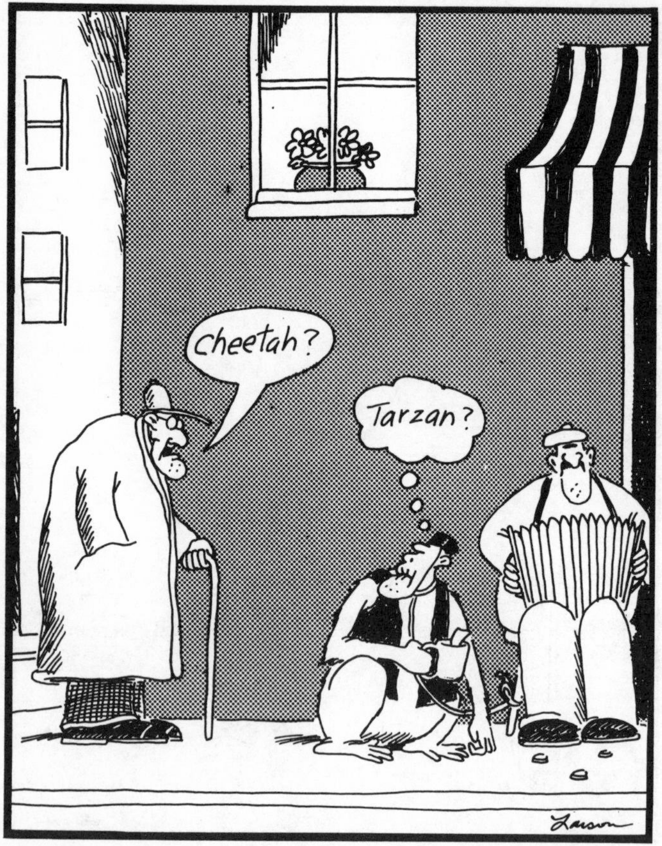
Cheetah?
Tarzan?
Larson

Their reunion was both brief and awkward — each still bearing the wounds from that ugly "Jane incident."

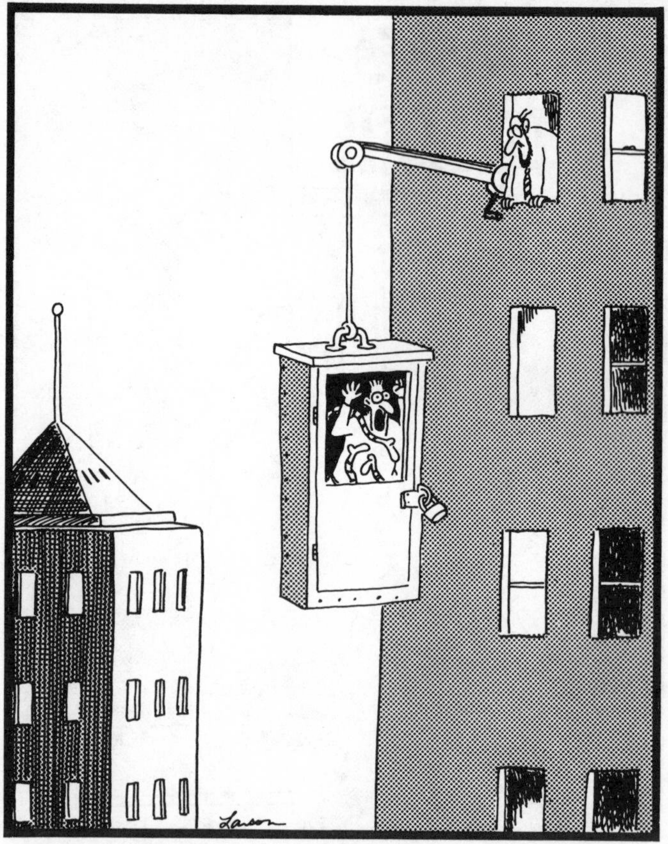
Larson

Professor Gallagher and his controversial technique of simultaneously confronting the fear of heights, snakes, and the dark.

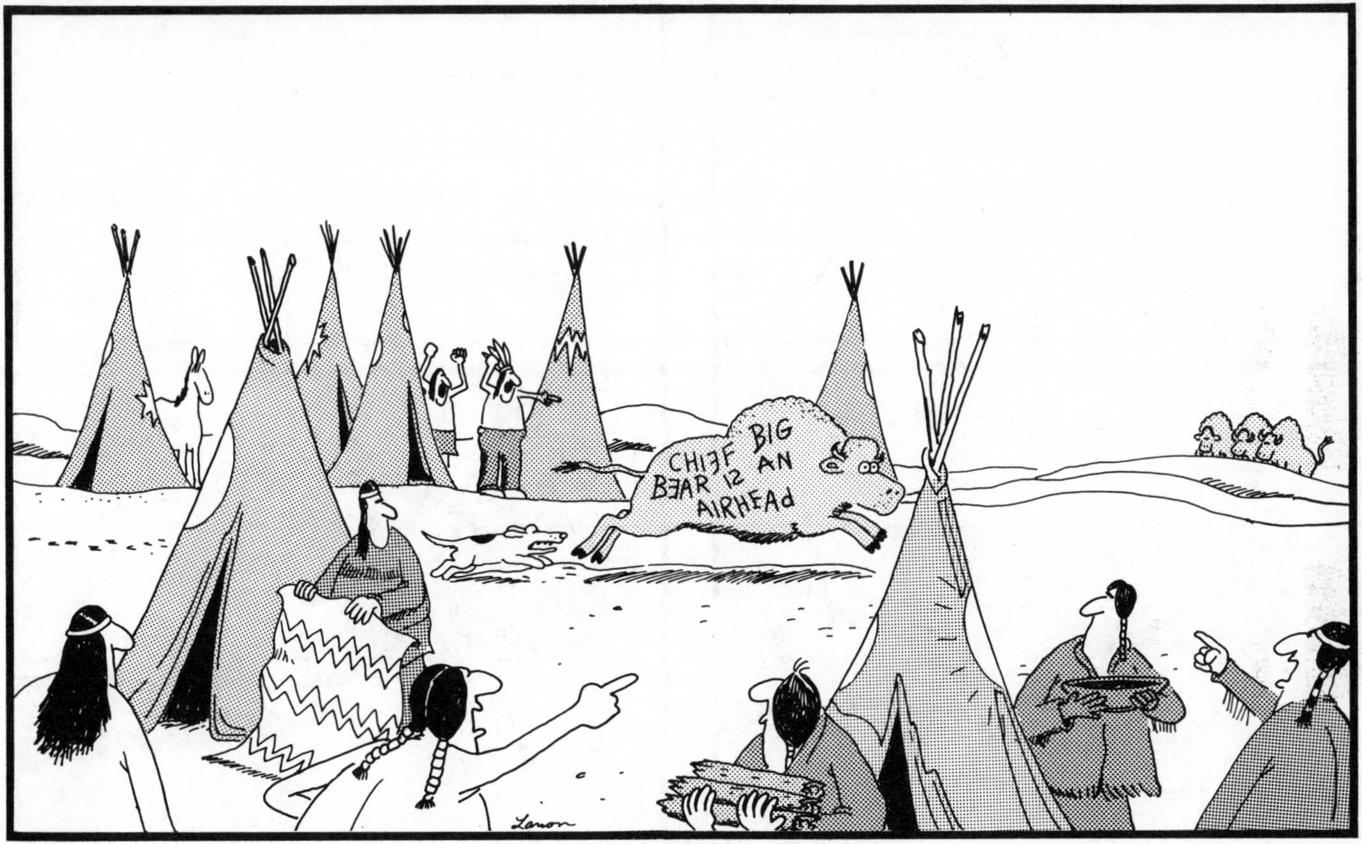
CHIEF BIG
BEAR IZ AN
AIRHEAd
Larson

Buffalo dares

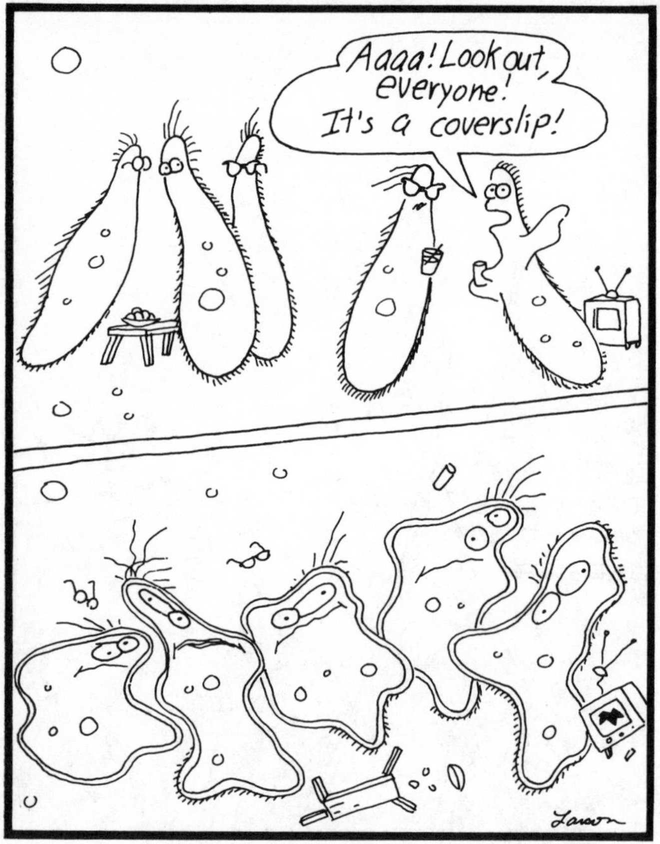
Aaaa! Look out, everyone! It's a coverslip!

Life on a microscope slide

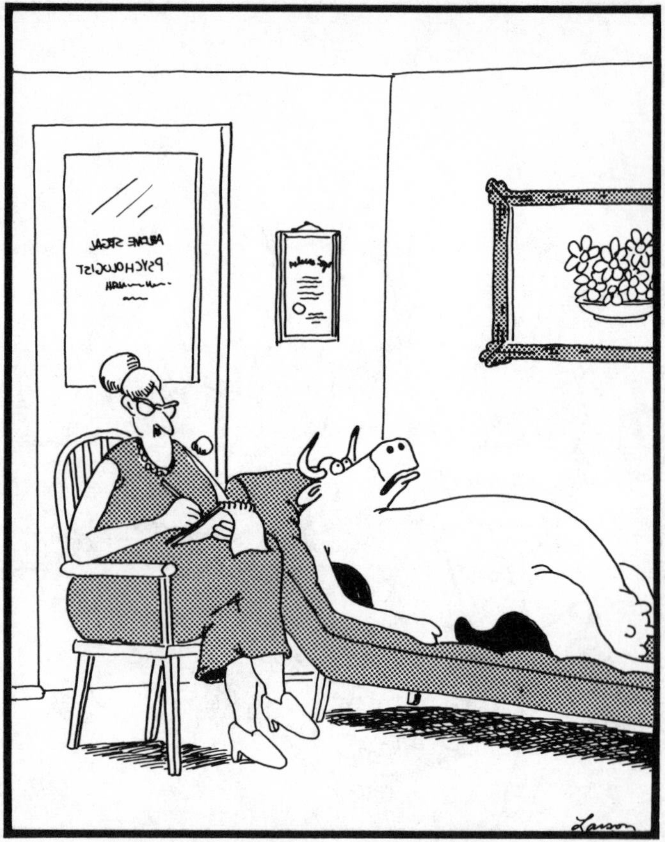

"Maybe it's *not* me, y'know? . . . Maybe it's the *rest* of the herd that's gone insane."

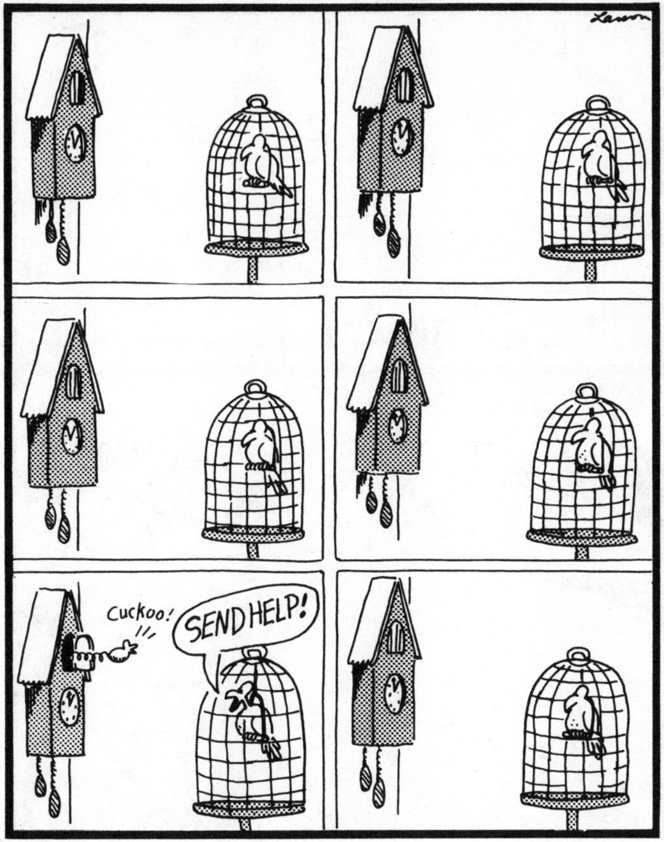
Larson
Cuckoo!
SEND HELP!

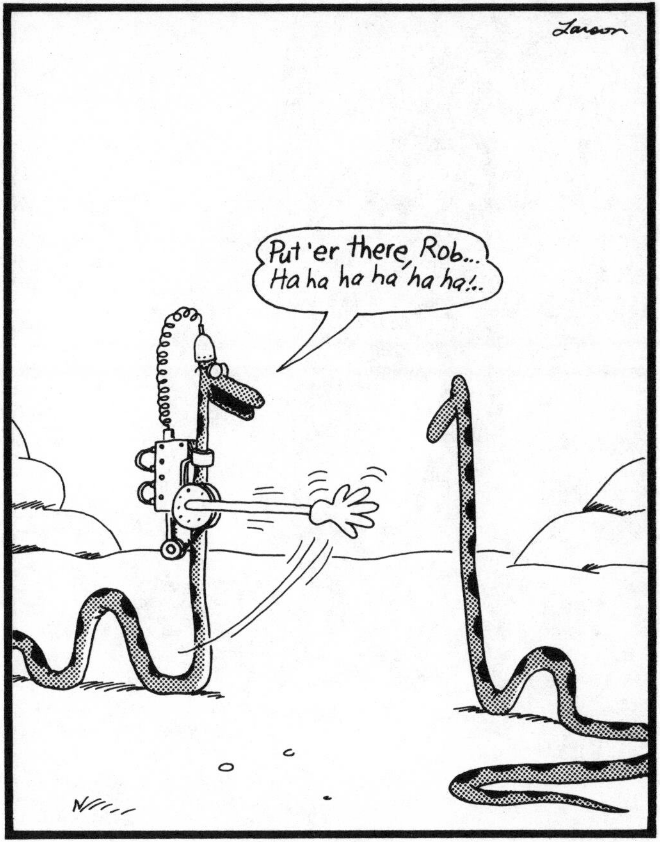
Larson
Put 'er there, Rob...
Ha ha ha ha ha ha!..

Snake inventors

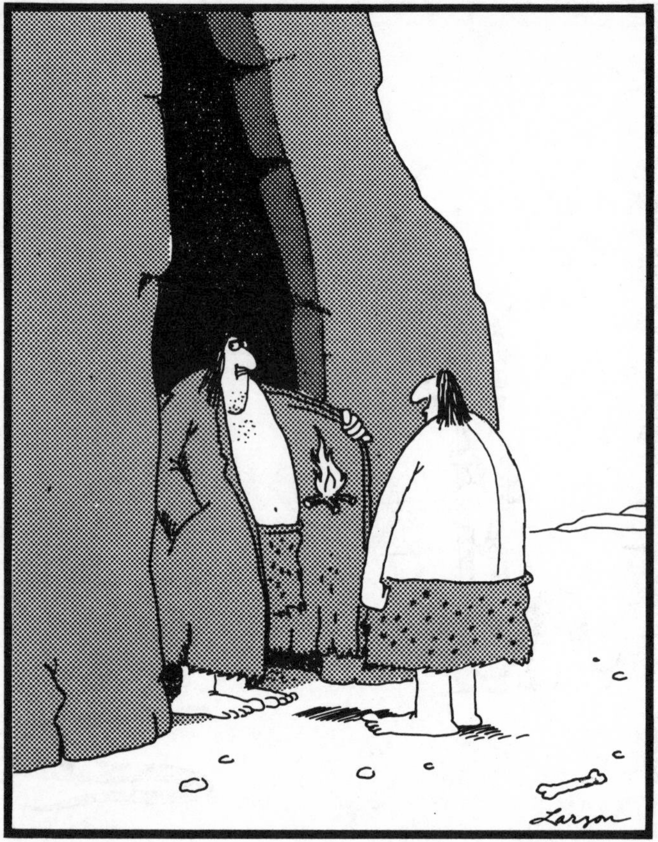
Larson

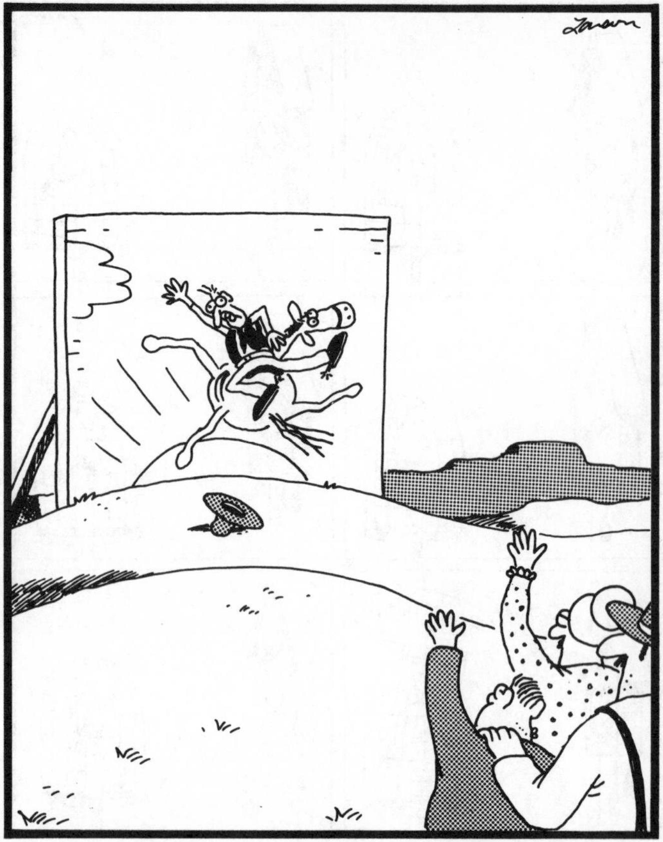
Larson

The embarrassment of riding off into a fake sunset

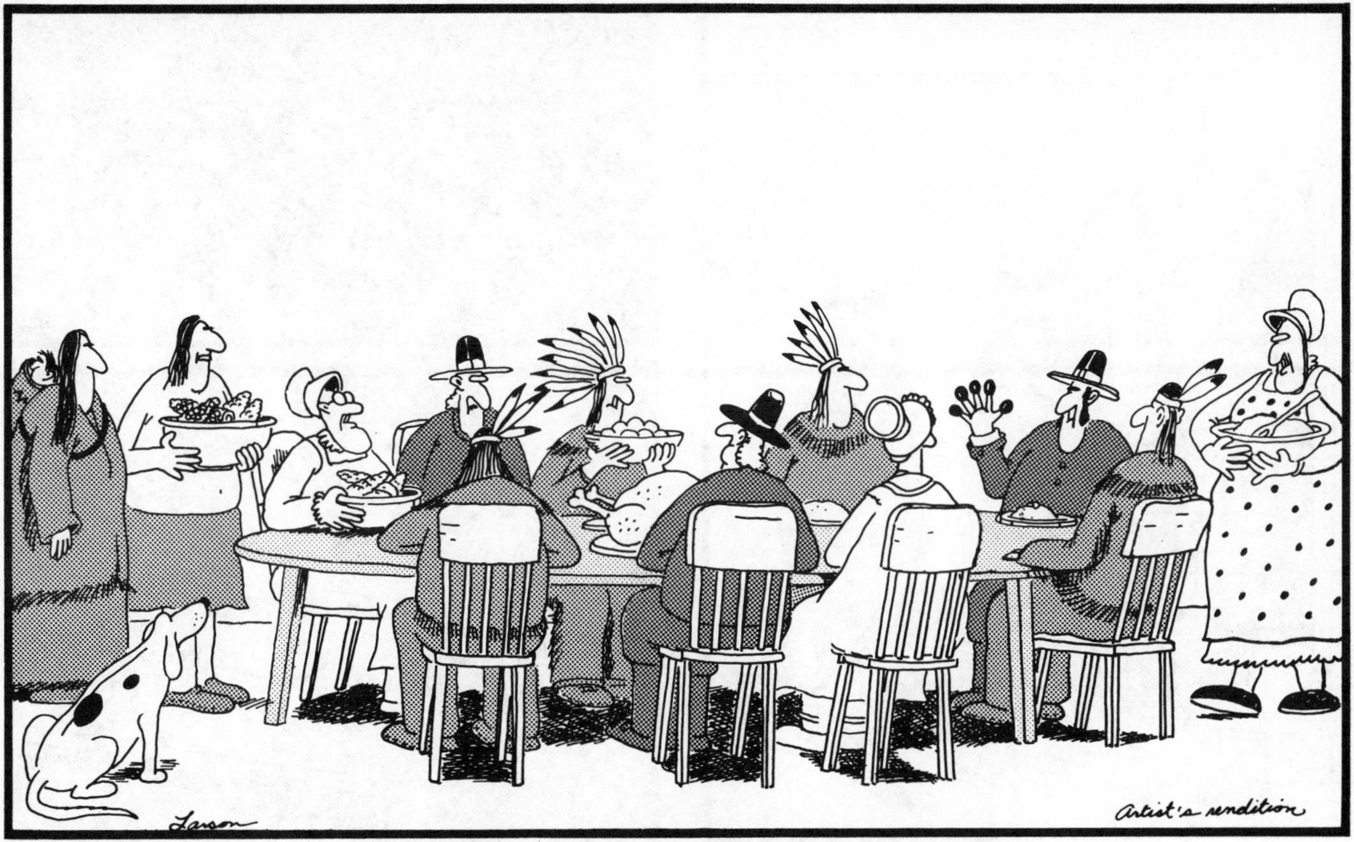
Larson
Artist's rendition

Thomas Sullivan, a blacksmith who attended the original Thanksgiving dinner, is generally credited as being the first person to stick olives on all his fingers.

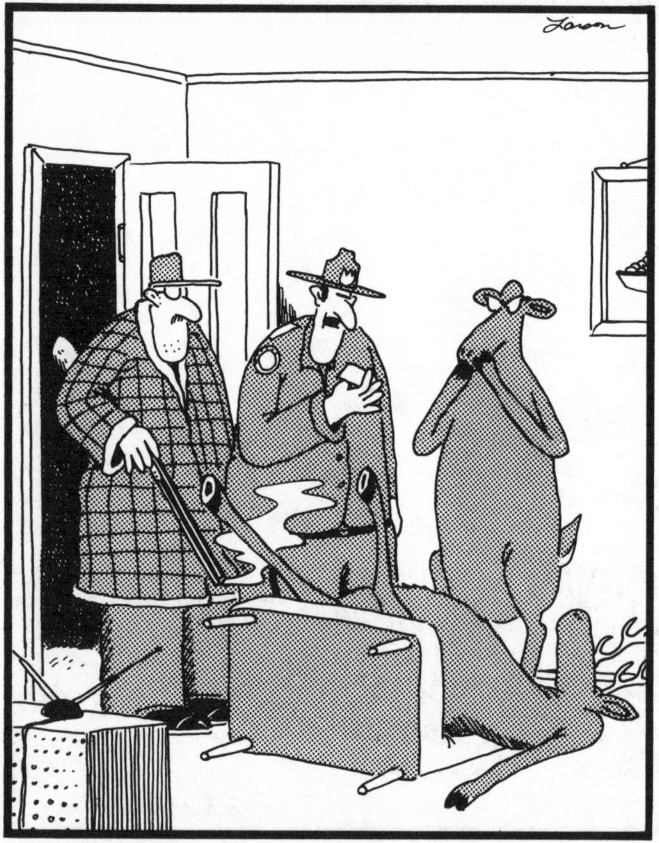
Larson

"I'm sorry, ma'am, but his license does check out and, after all, your husband *was* in season. Remember, just because he knocks doesn't mean you have to let him in."

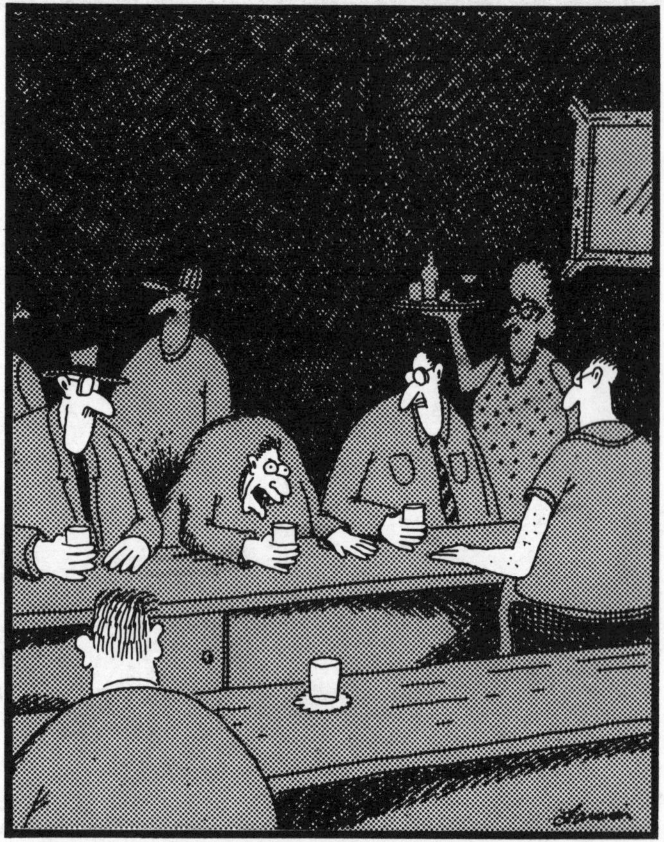

"Yeah. My boss don't appreciate me either. To him I'm just a gofer. 'Igor! Go for dead bodies! . . . Igor! Go for brains! . . . Igor! Go for dead bodies!' I dunno — give me another beer."

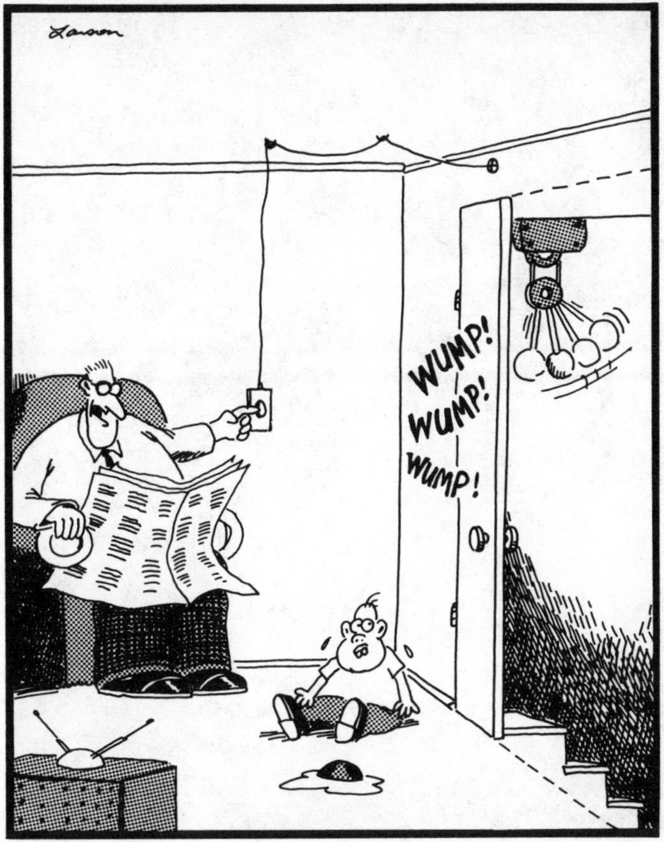
Larson
WUMP!
WUMP!
WUMP!

"Uh-oh, Danny. Sounds like the monster in the basement has heard you crying again. . . . Let's be reaaaal quiet and hope he goes away."

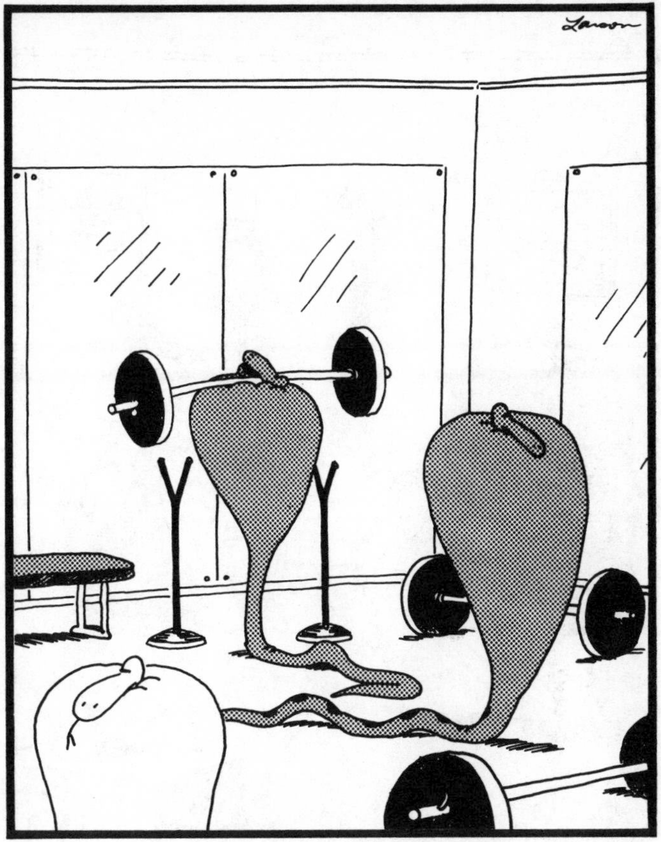
Larson

Snake weight-rooms

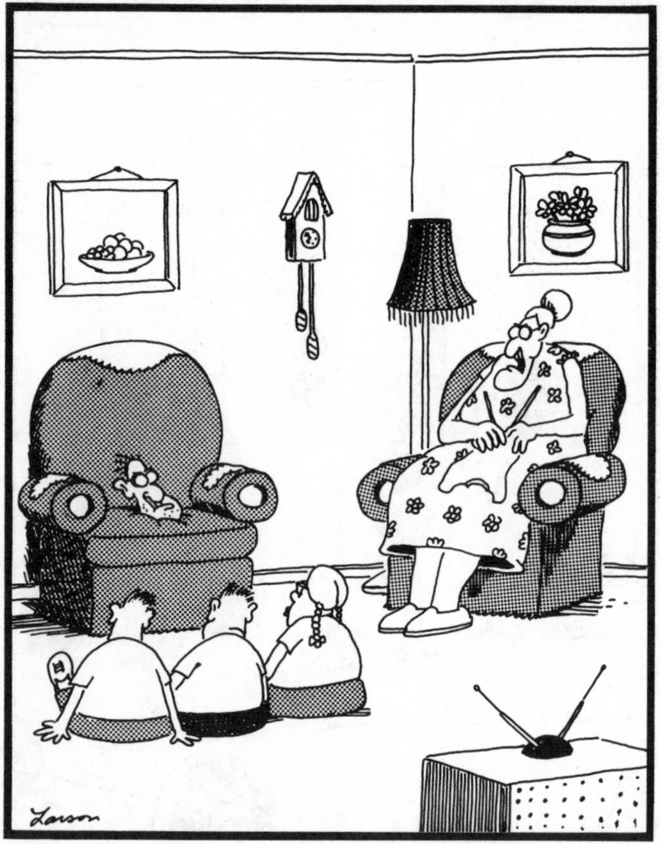

"For heaven's sake, Henry, tell the kids a *pleasant* story for once — they don't always have to hear the one about your head."

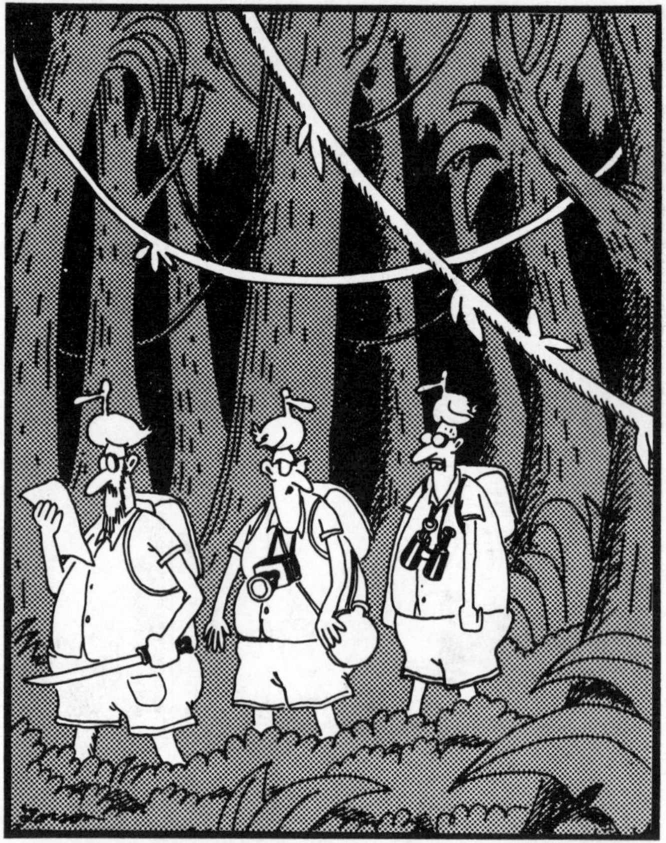

Onward they pushed, through the thick, steamy jungle, separately ruing the witch doctor's parting words: "Before you leave this valley, each of you will be wearing a duck."

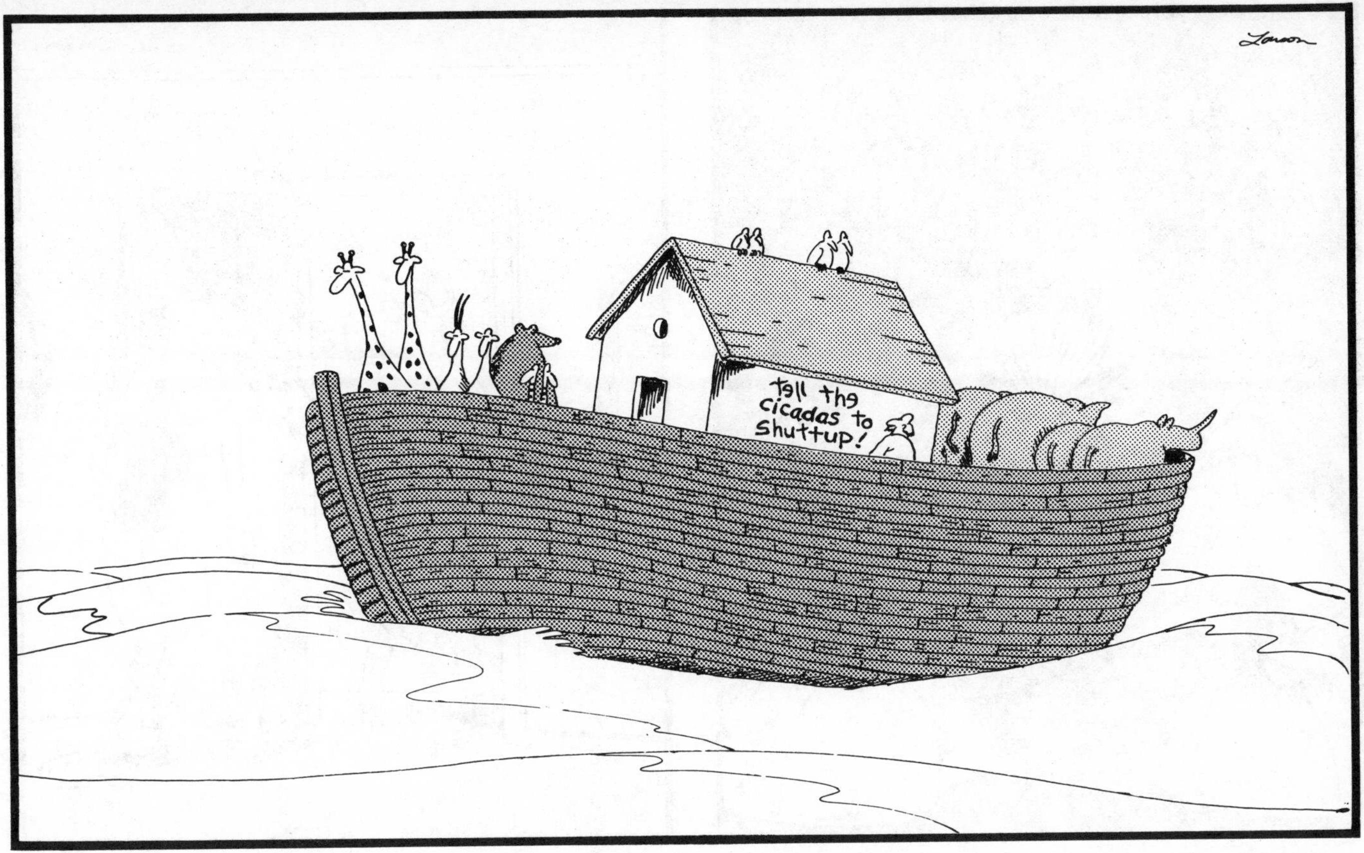
tell the
cicadas to
shuttup!

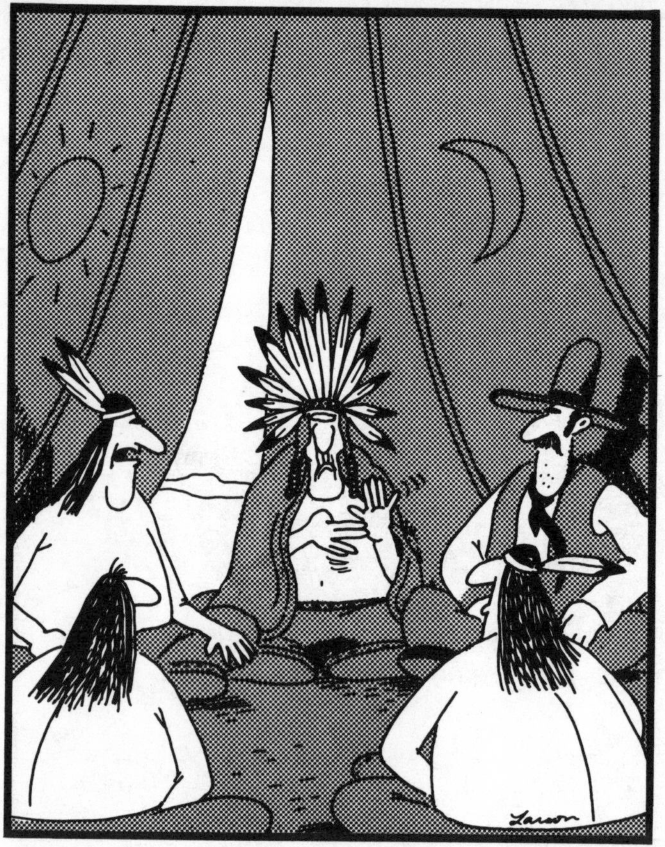
Larson

"Chief say, 'Someone . . . here . . . walk . . . through . . . buffalo . . . field.'"

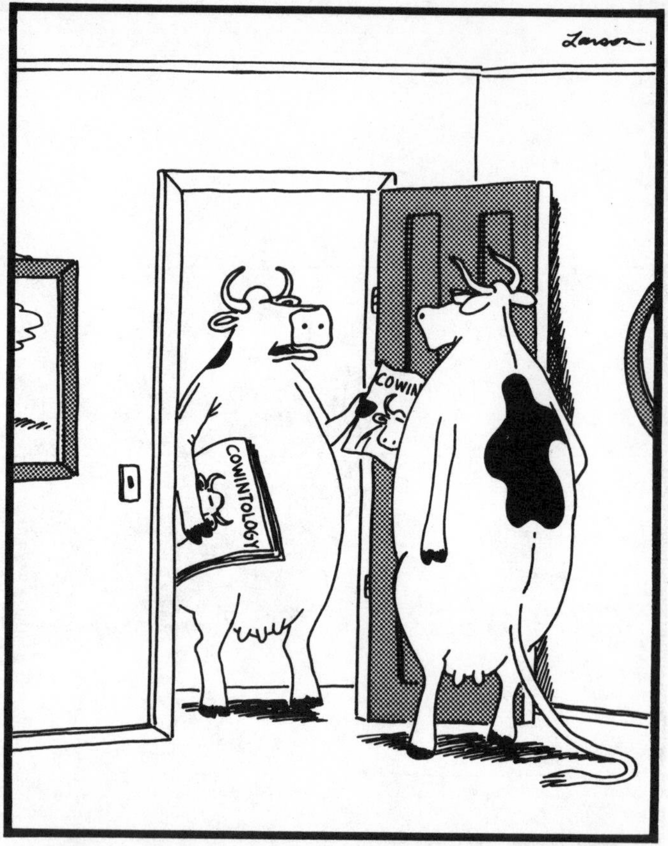
Larson
COWIN
COWINTOLOGY

"Listen — just take one of our brochures and see what we're all about. . . . In the meantime, you may wish to ask yourself, 'Am I a happy cow?'"

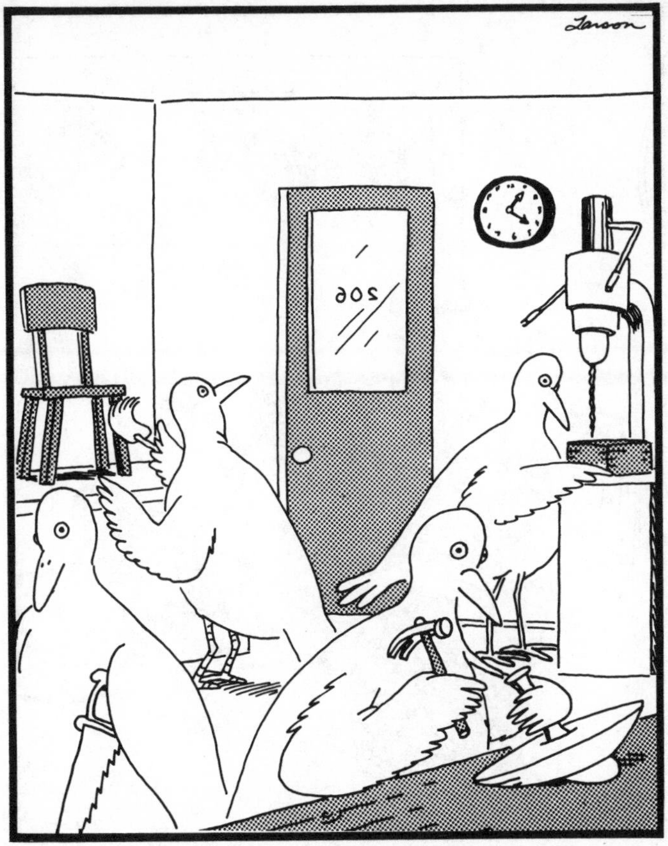
Larson

Non-singing canaries have to take wood shop.

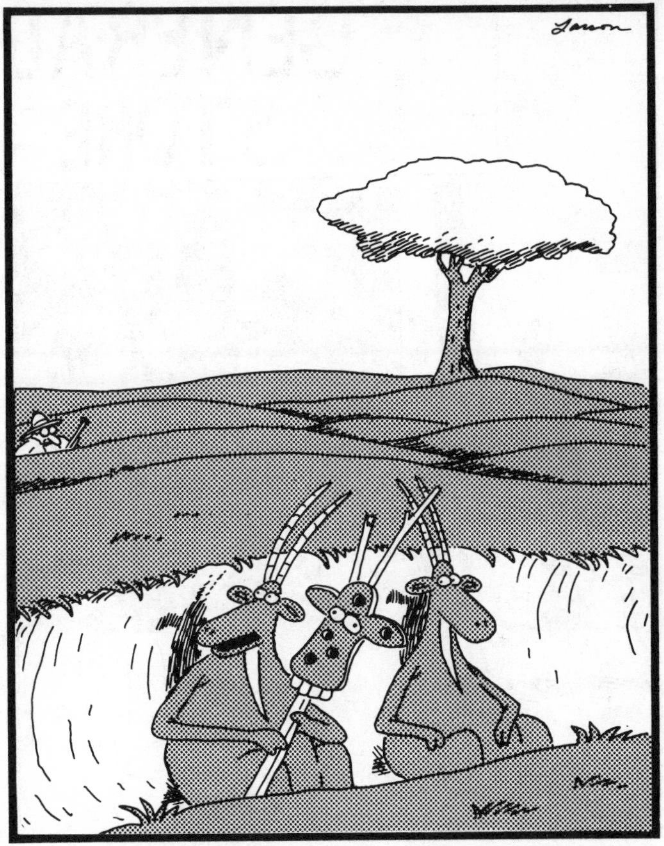
Larson

"He's got one shot left, Murray — and then he's *ours*!"

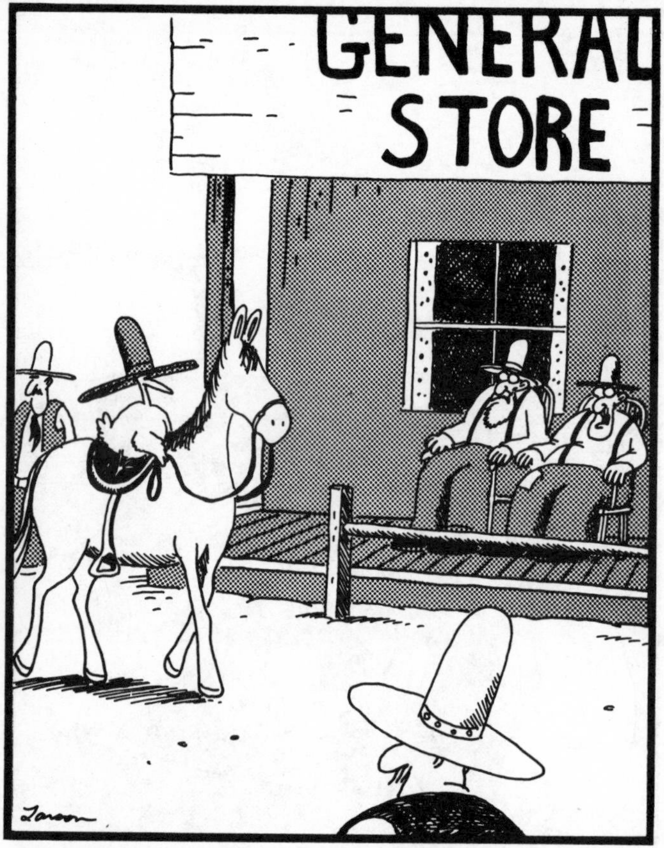
GENERAL
STORE
Larson

"Somethin's up, Jake. . . . That's Ben Potter's horse, all right, but ain't that Henry Morgan's chicken ridin' him?"

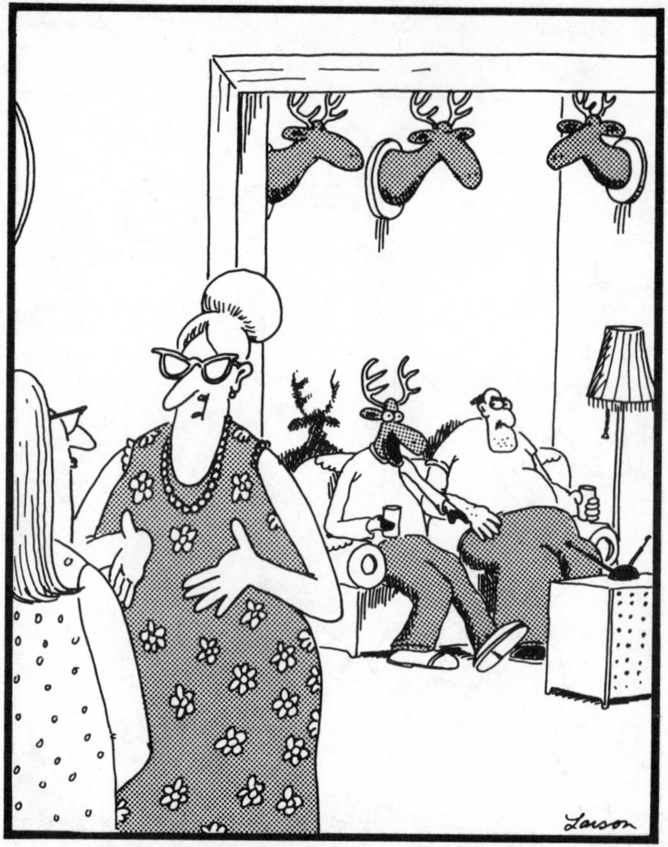
Larson

"It's this new boyfriend, dear. . . . I'm just afraid one day your father's going to up and blow him away."

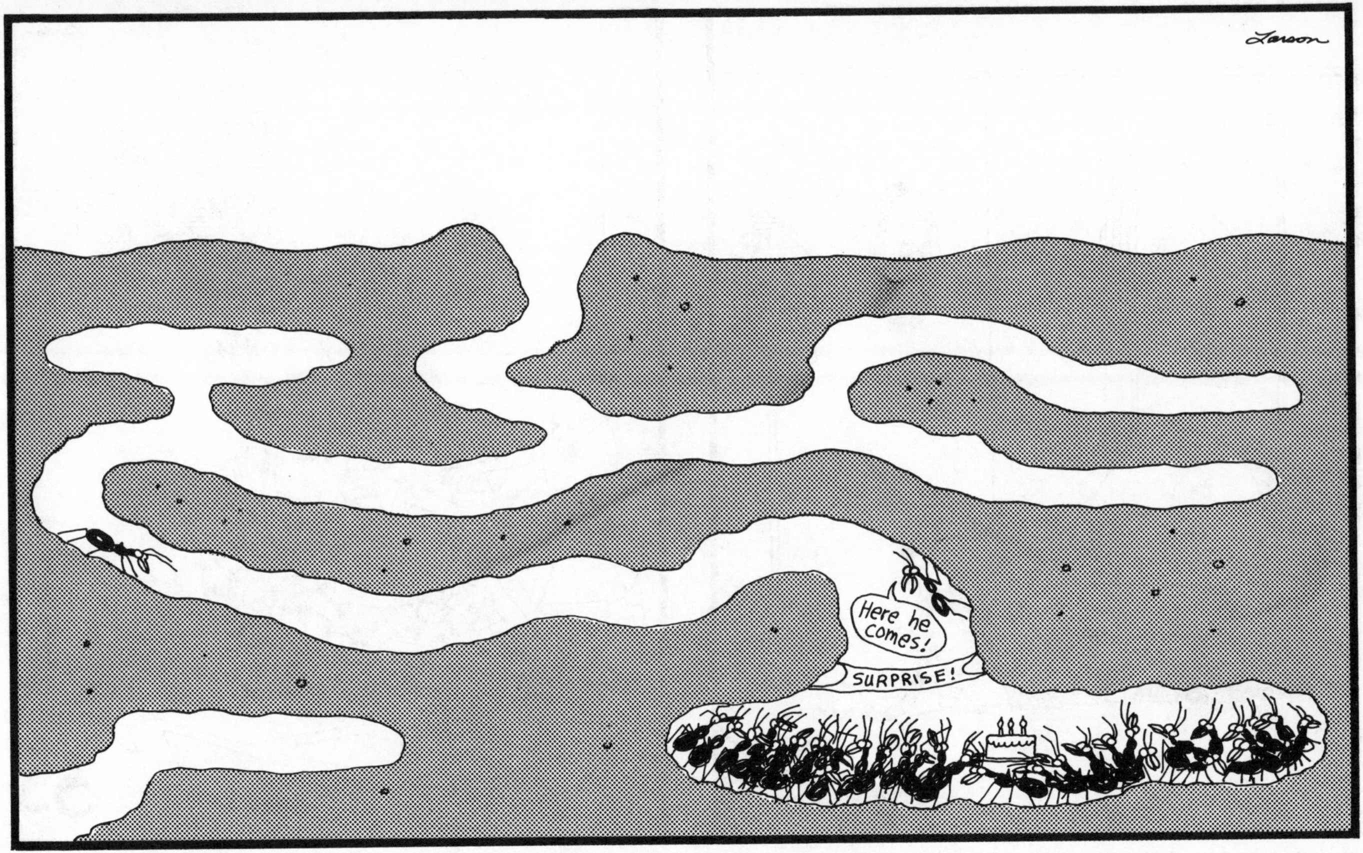
Larson
Here he comes!
SURPRISE!

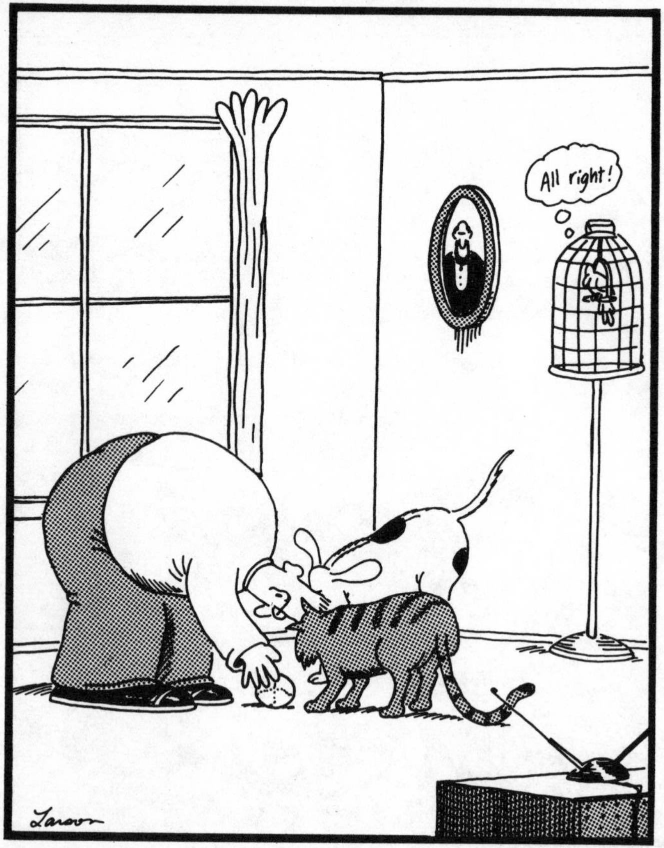
All right!
Larson

Simultaneously all three went for the ball, and the coconut-like sound of their heads colliding secretly delighted the bird.

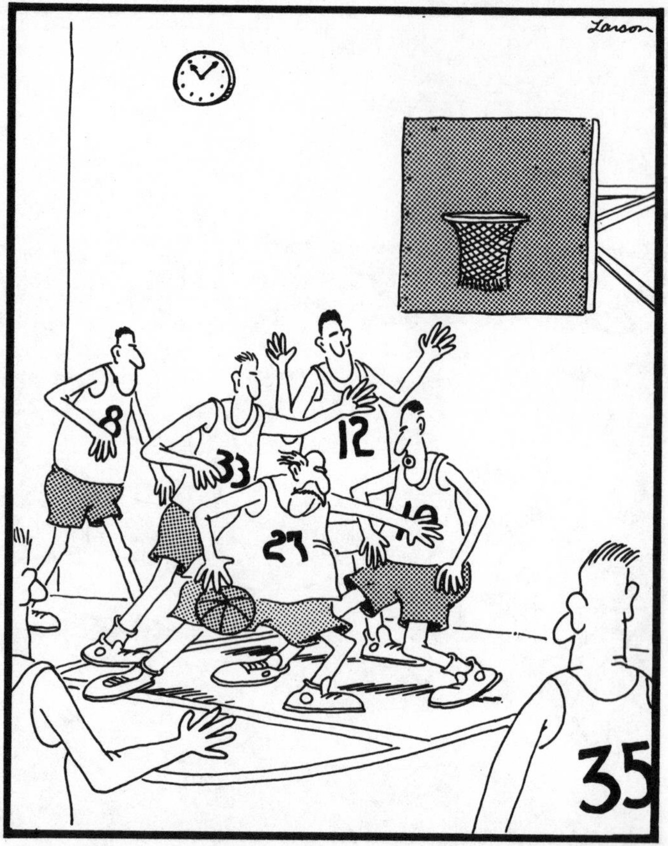
Larson

Unbeknownst to most historians, Einstein started down the road of professional basketball before an ankle injury diverted him into science.

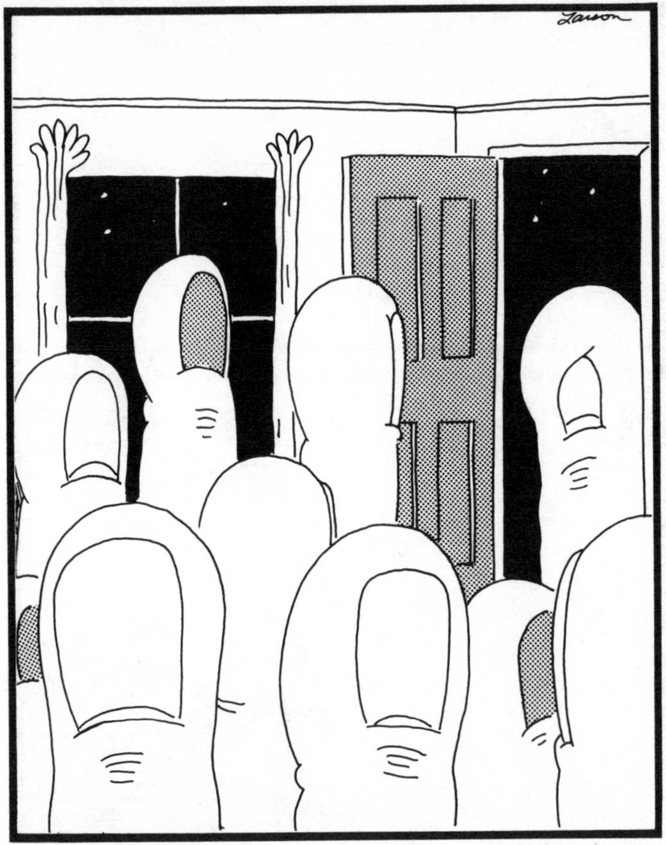
Larson

Suddenly, everyone turned and looked — there, standing in the doorway, was one wretched, mean-looking ingrown.

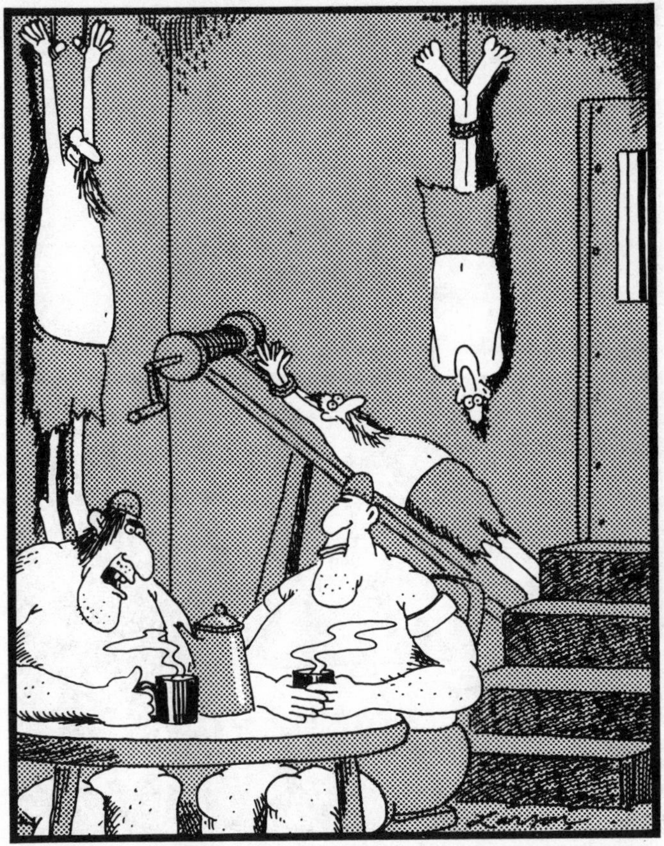
Larson

"You know, Russell, you're a great torturer. I mean, you can make a man scream for mercy in nothing flat . . . but boy, you sure can't make a good cup of coffee."

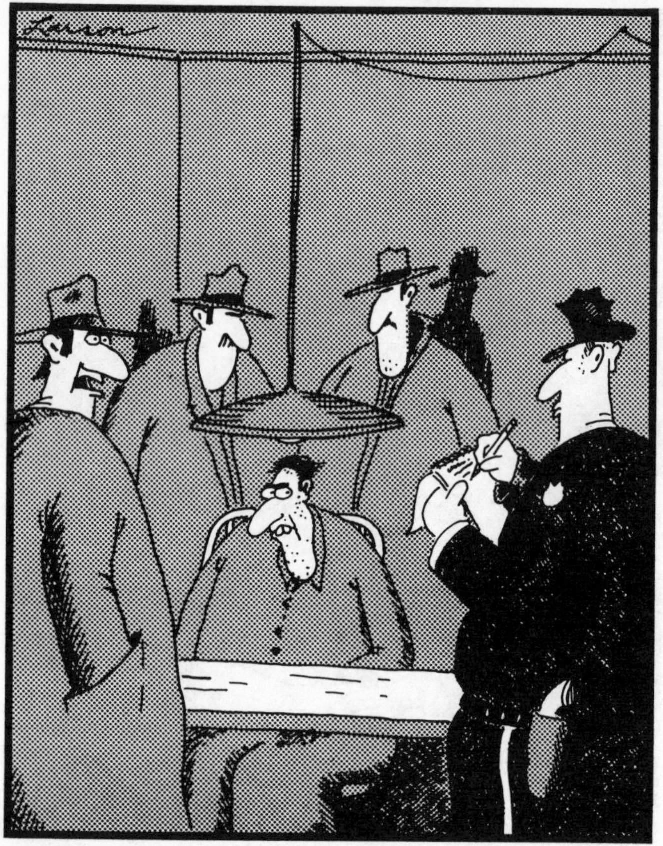
Larson

"You idiot! Don't write that down — his name ain't Puddin' Tame!"

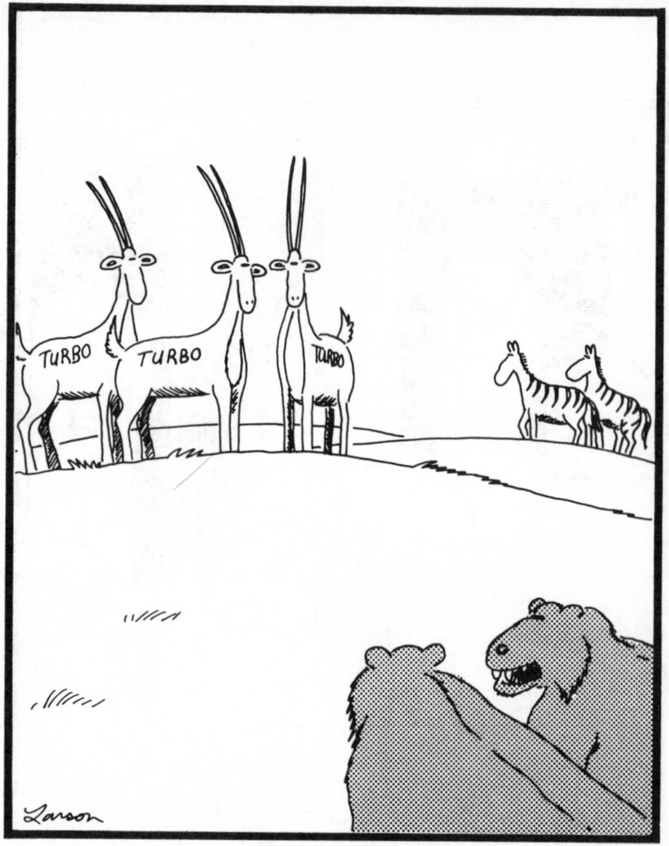
TURBO
TURBO
TURBO
Larson

"Forget these guys."

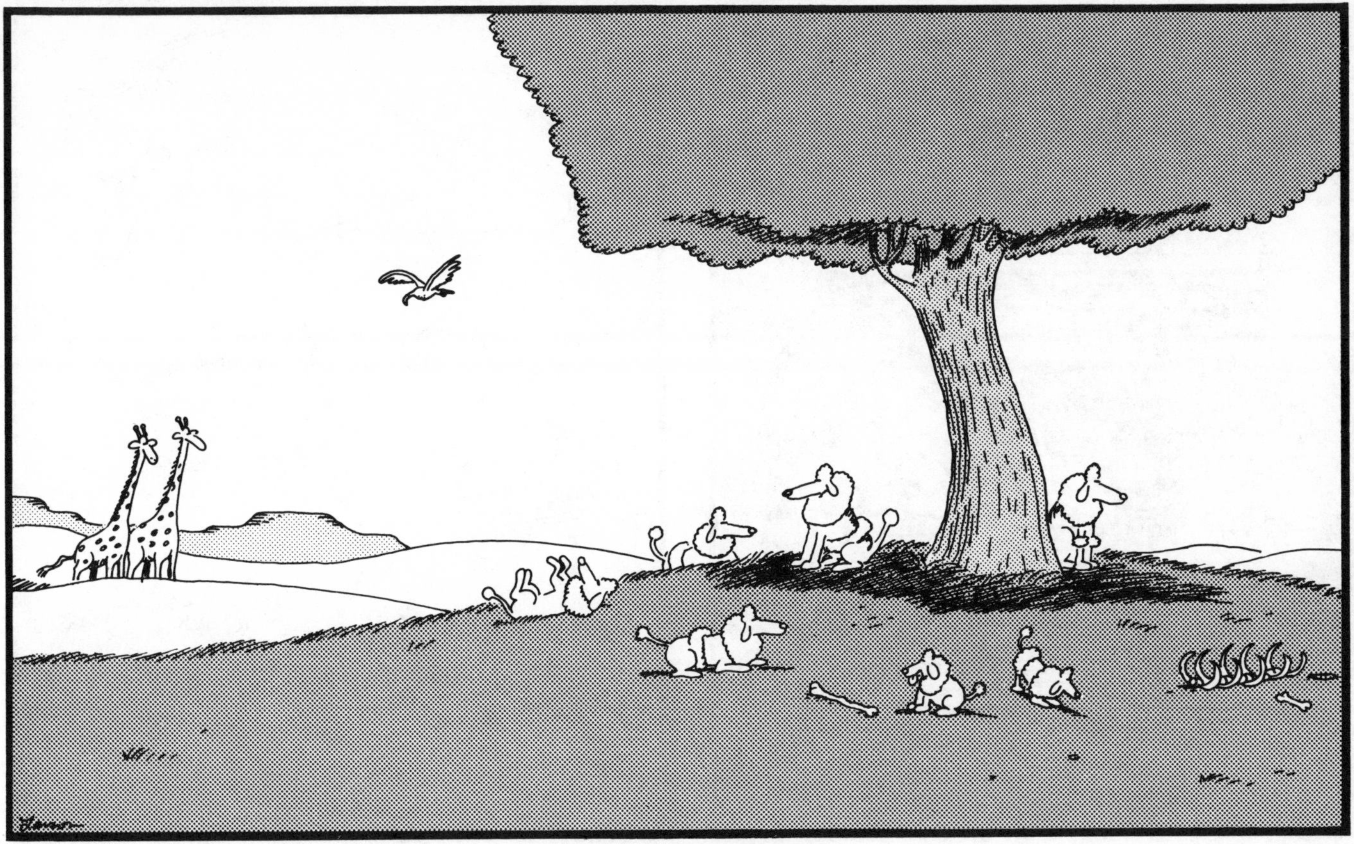

Poodles of the Serengeti

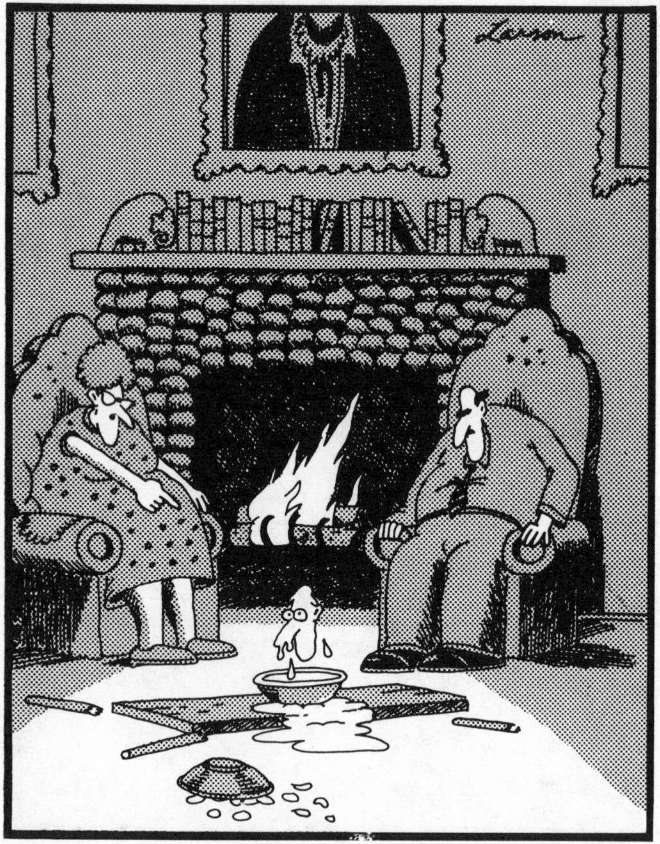

The ghost of Baron Rudolph von Guggenheim, 16th-century nobleman murdered by the Countess Rowena DuBois and her lover (believed to be the Duke of Norwood), falls into Edna's bean dip.

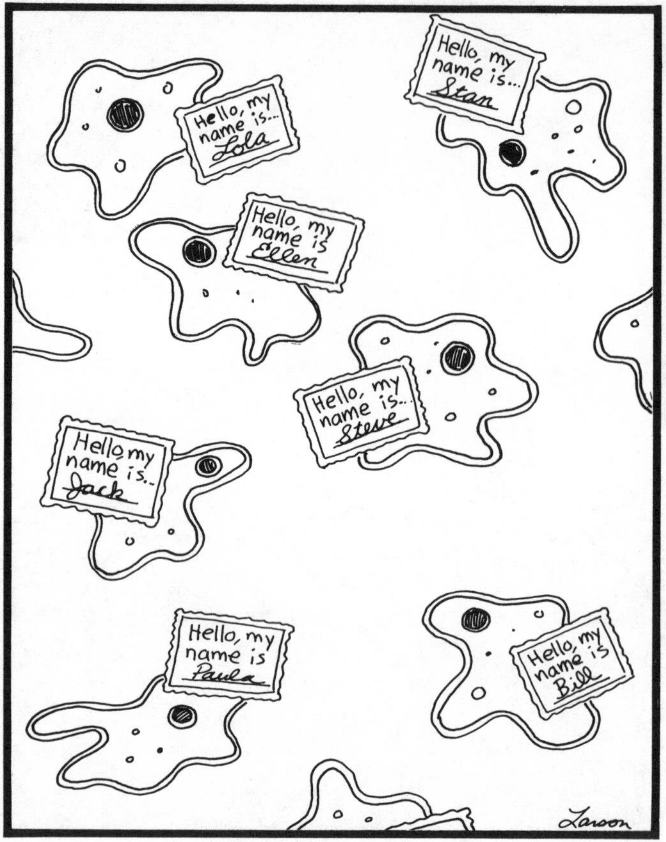

Hello, my name is... Stan
Hello, my name is... Lola
Hello, my name is Ellen
Hello, my name is... Steve
Hello, my name is... Jack
Hello, my name is Paula
Hello, my name is Bill

Amoeba conventions

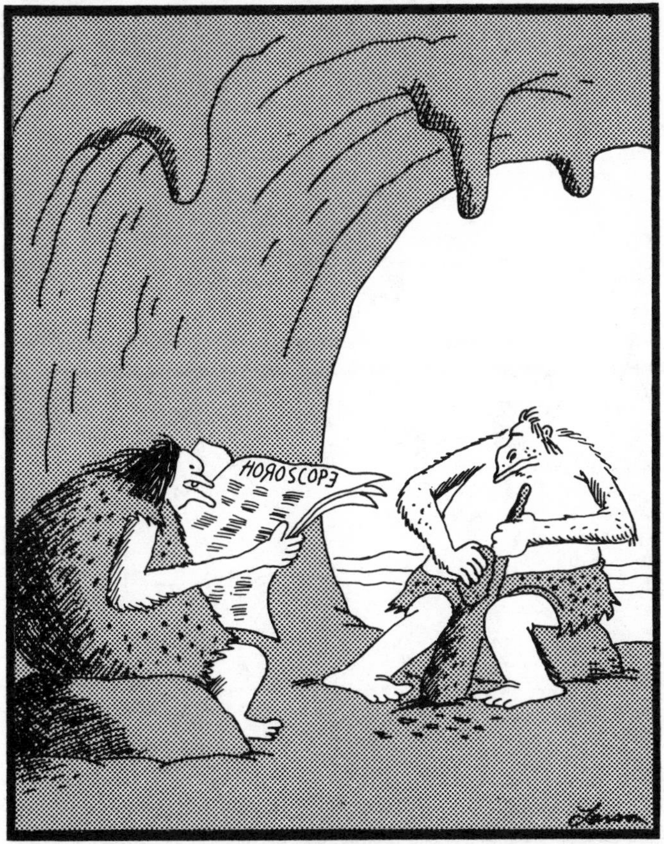
HOROSCOPE

"'You have a small capacity for reason, some basic tool-making skills, and the use of a few simple words.' . . . Yep. That's you."

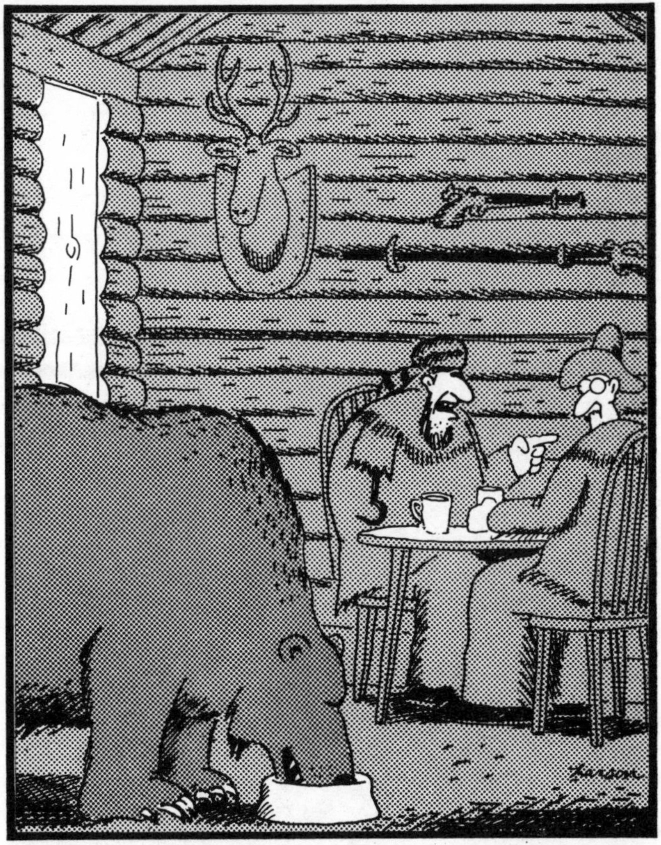

"Raised the ol' girl from a cub, I did. . . . 'Course, we had to get a few things straight between us. She don't try to follow me into town anymore, and I don't try and take her food bowl away 'til she's done."

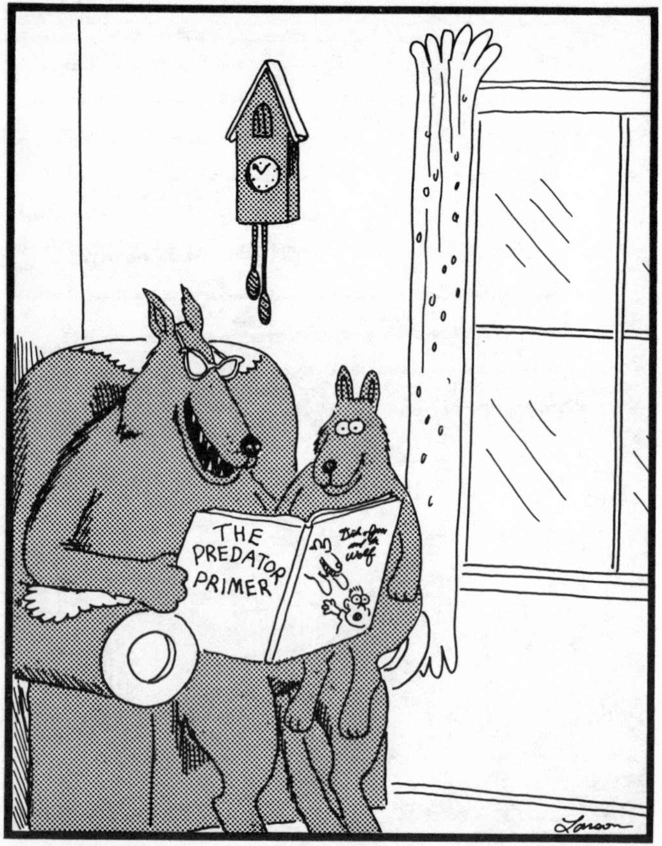
THE PREDATOR PRIMER
Larson

"See Dick run. See Jane run. Run run run. See the wolves chase Dick and Jane. Chase chase chase. . . ."

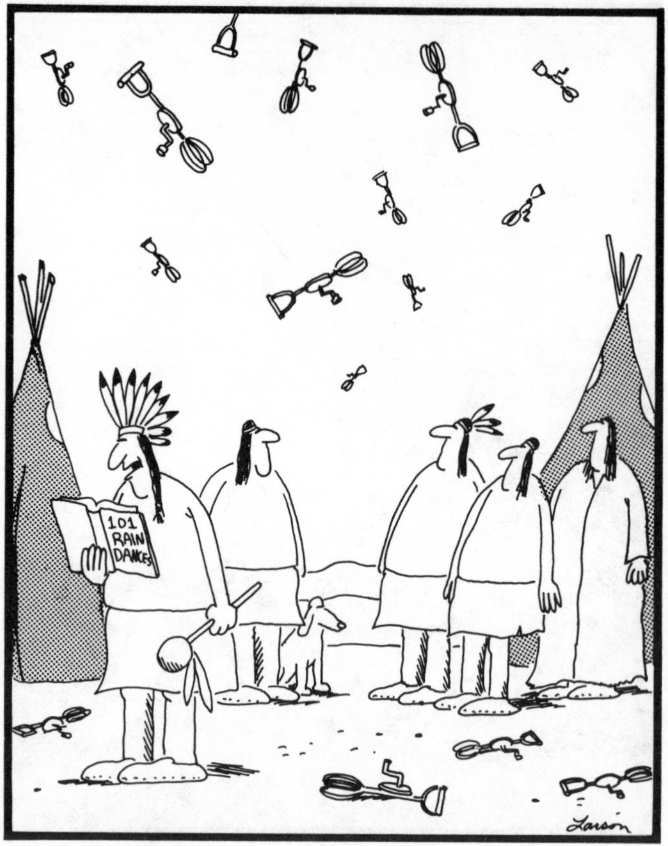
101 RAIN DANCES
Larson

"Oh! *Four* steps to the left and *then* three to the right! . . . What kind of a dance was *I* doing?"

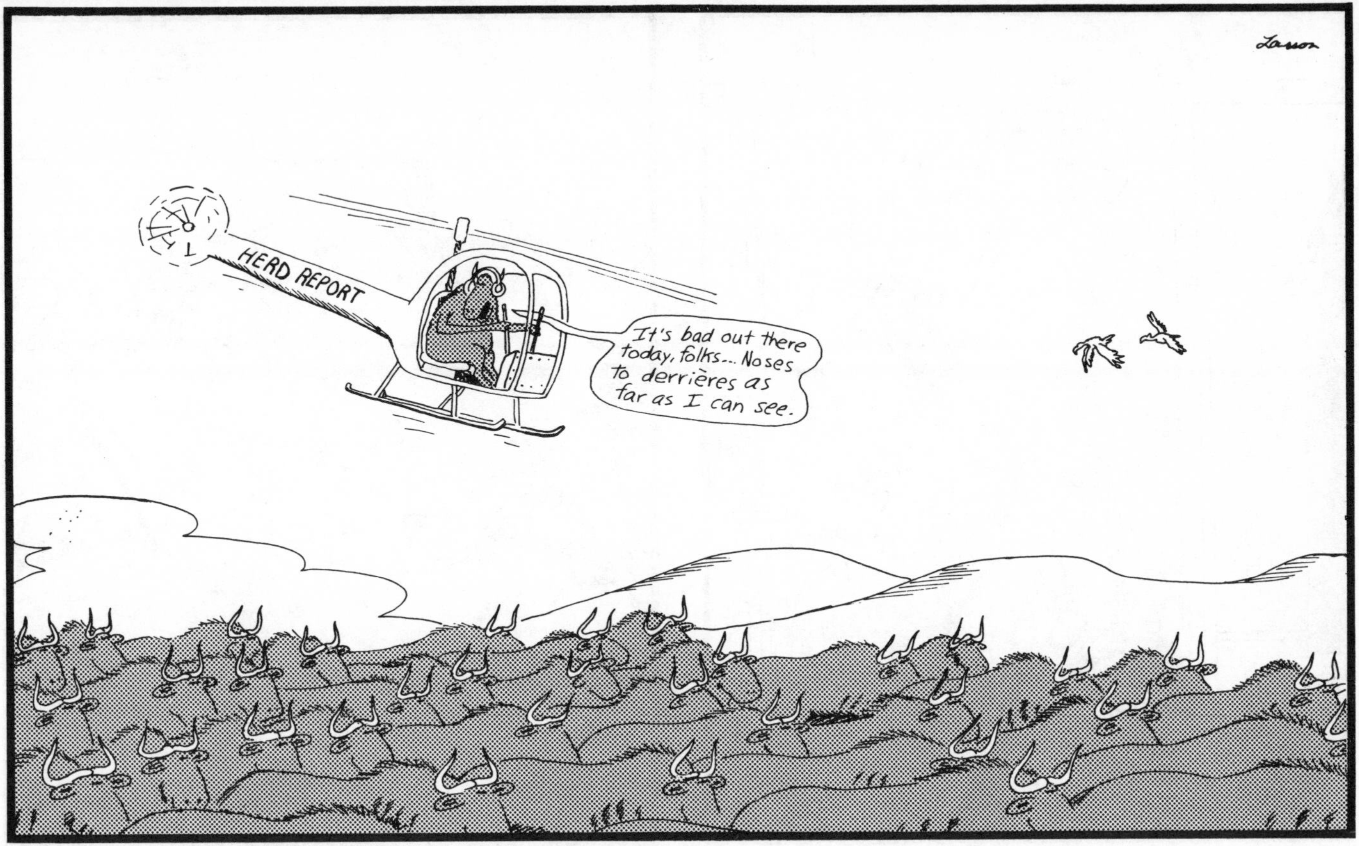
Larson
HERD REPORT
It's bad out there today, folks... Noses to derrières as far as I can see.

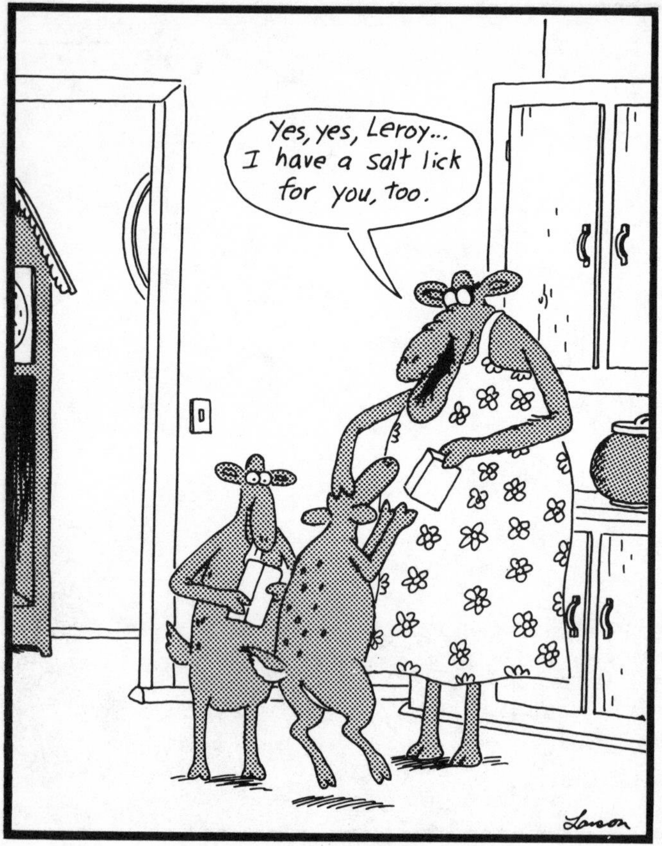
Yes, yes, Leroy...
I have a salt lick
for you, too.
Larson

Deer grandmothers

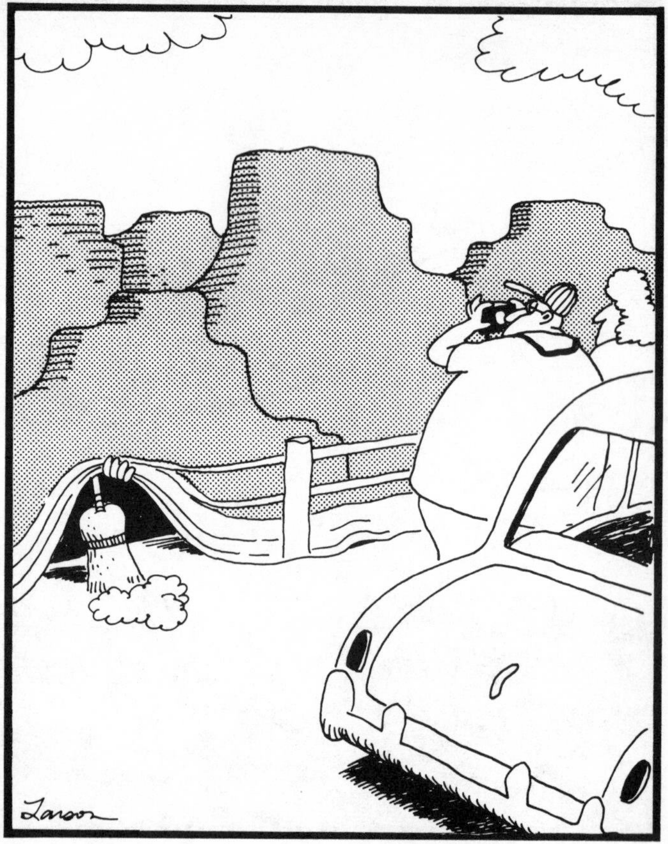
Larson

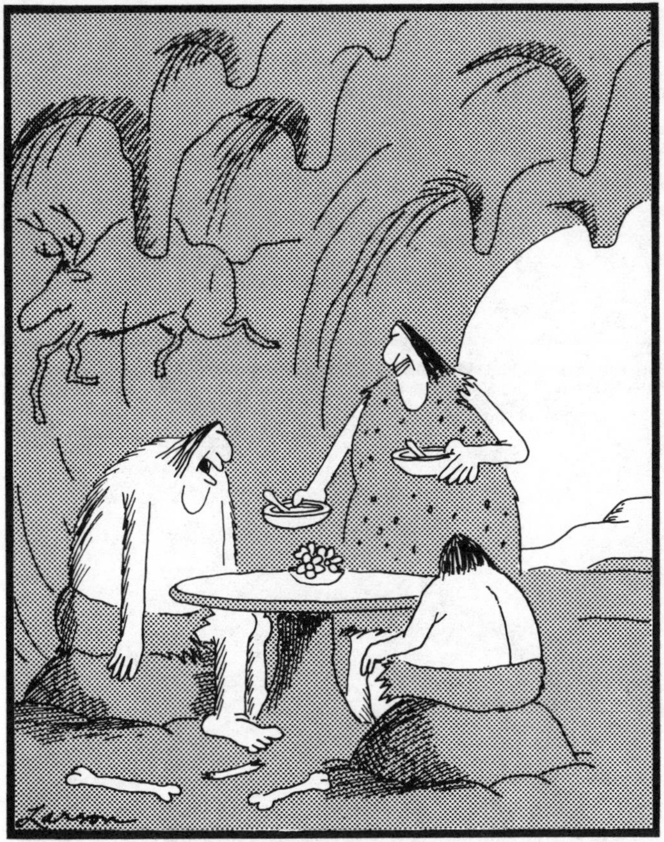

"Primordial soup again?"

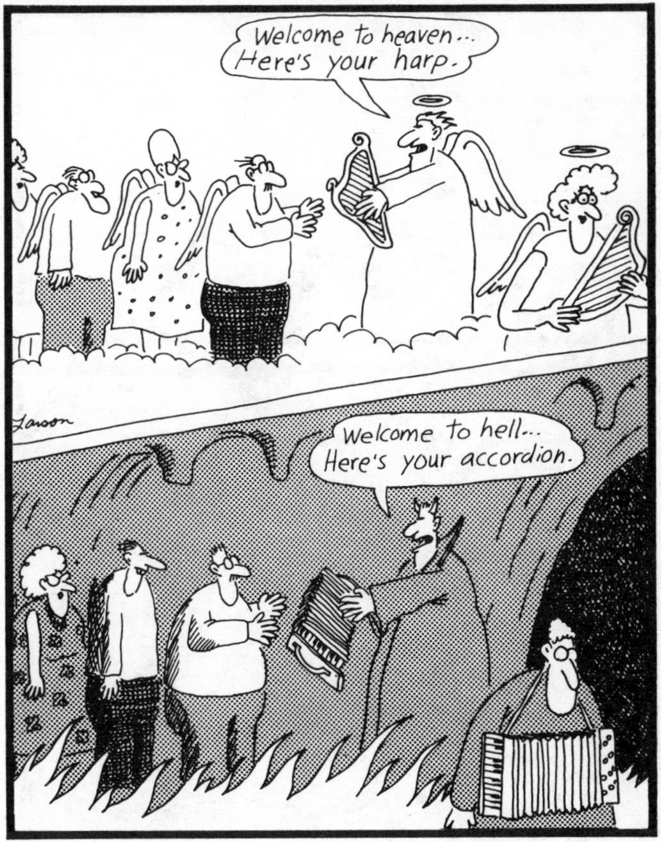
Welcome to heaven...
Here's your harp.
Welcome to hell...
Here's your accordion.

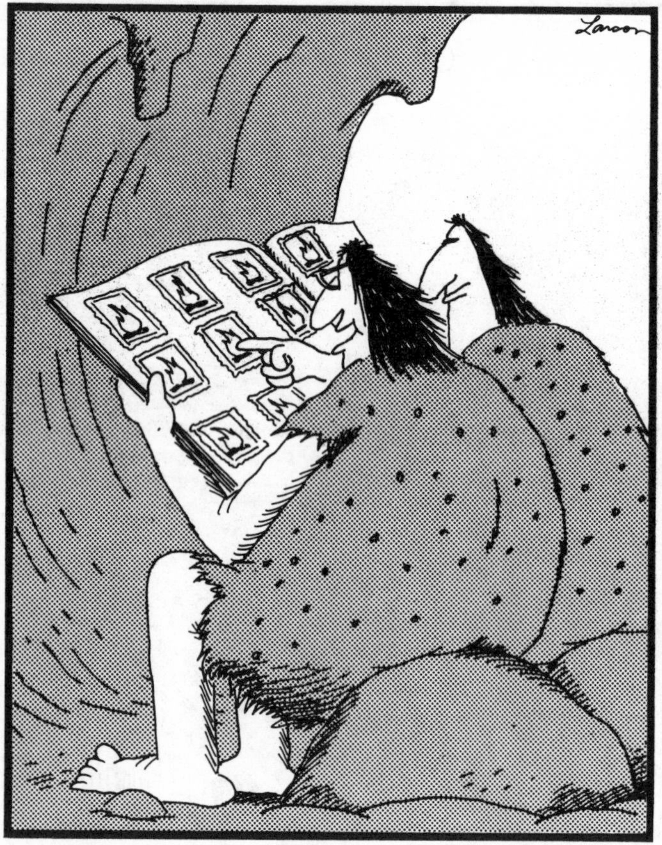
Larson

"Ooo! Now here's a nice one we built last fall."

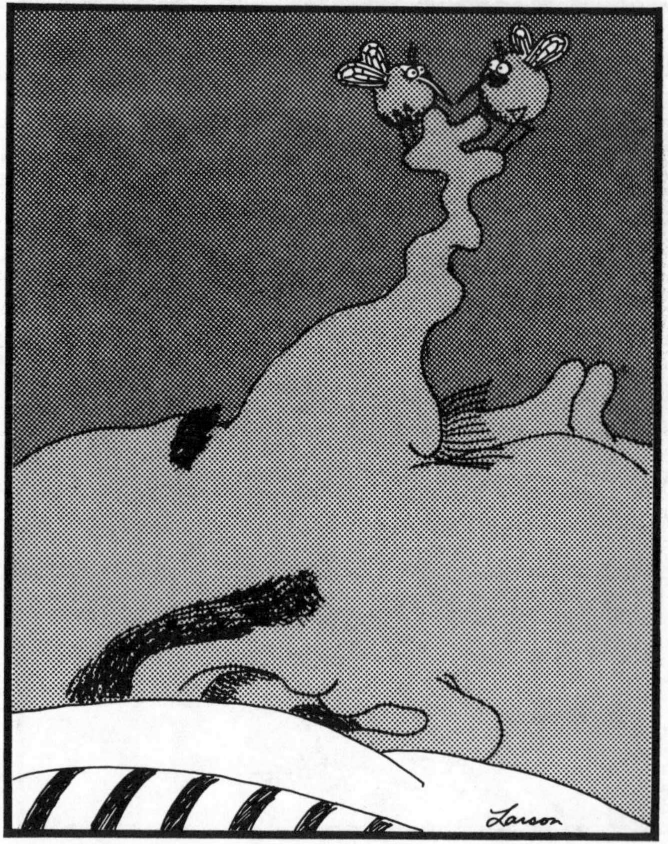
Larson

"Well, that about does it for the nose — I'm starting to hit cartilage."

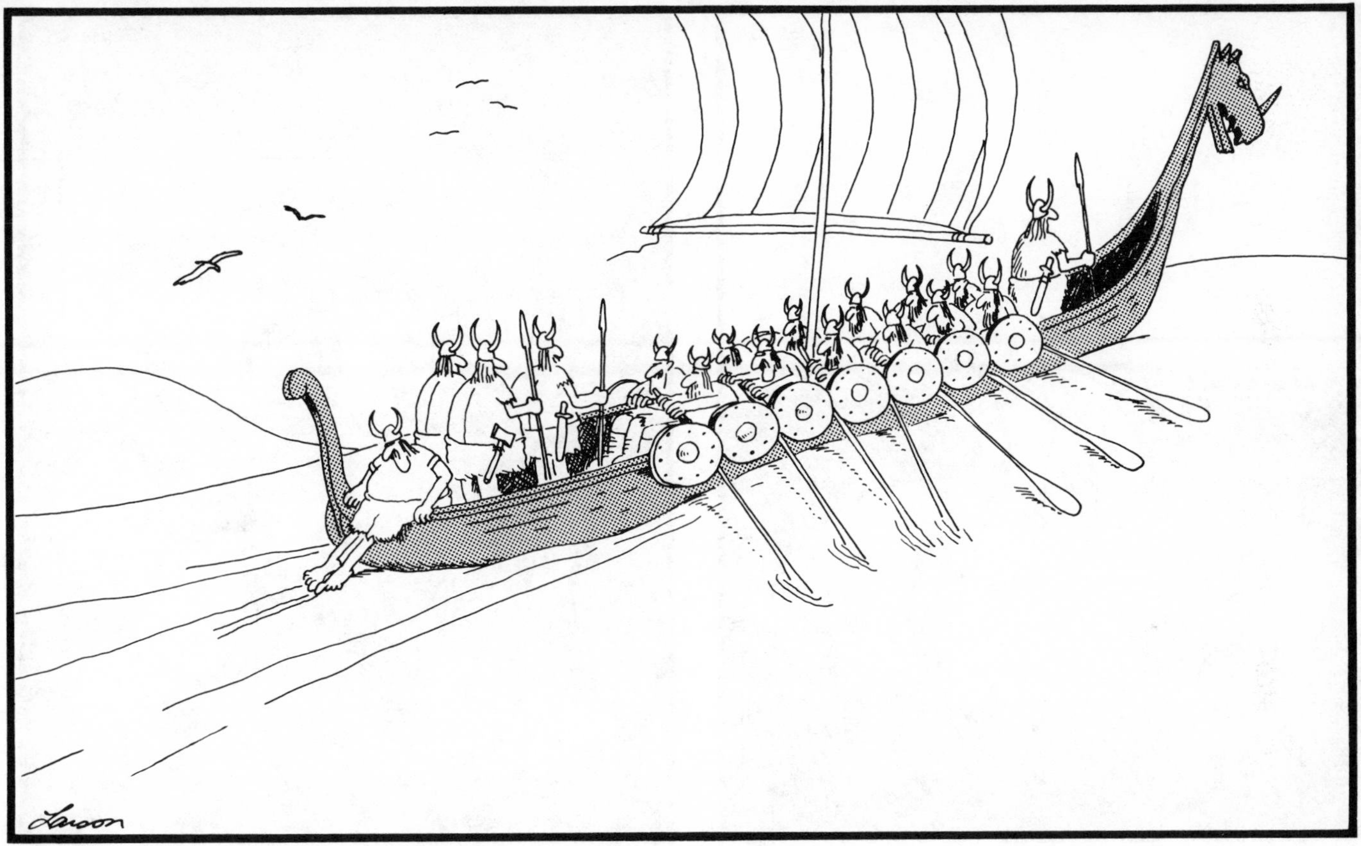
Larson

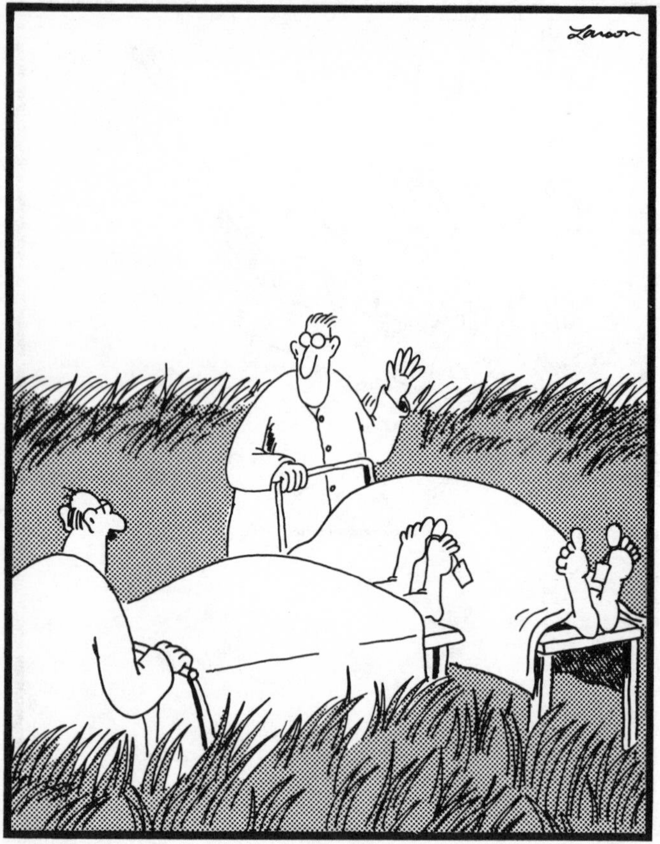

When a body meets a body comin' through the rye . . .

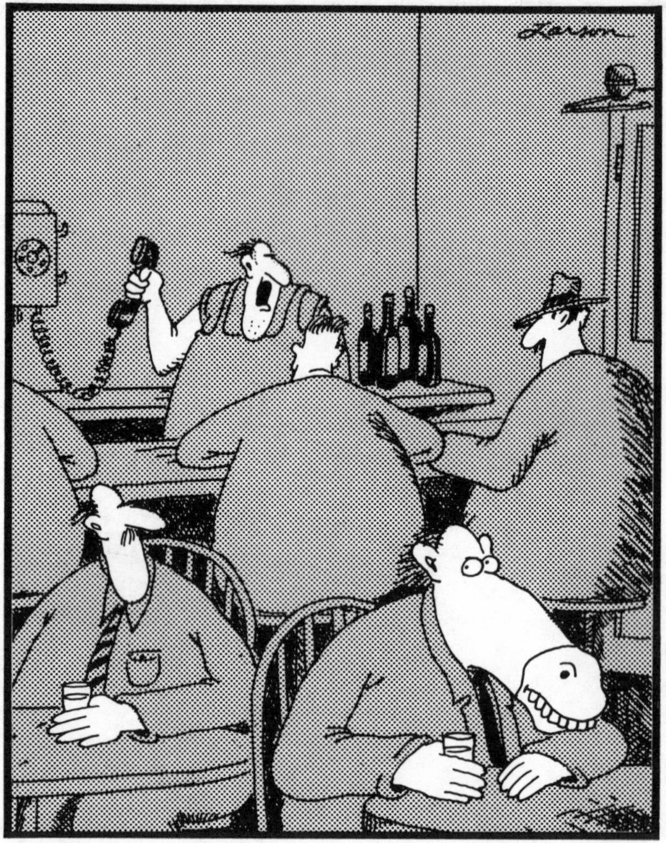

"Horse! . . . Is there a man called 'Horse' in here?"

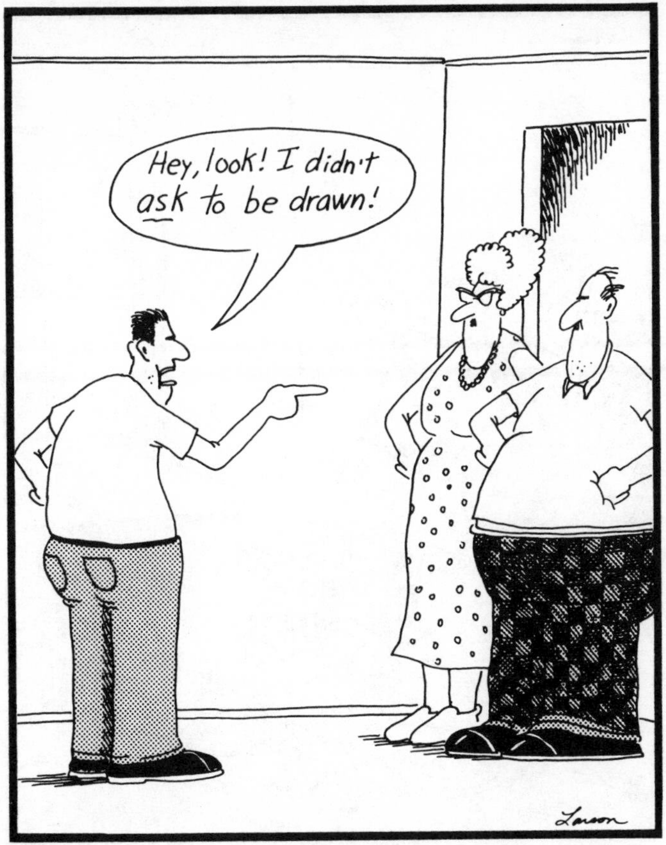

Hey, look! I didn't ask to be drawn!
Larson

Cartoon teen-agers

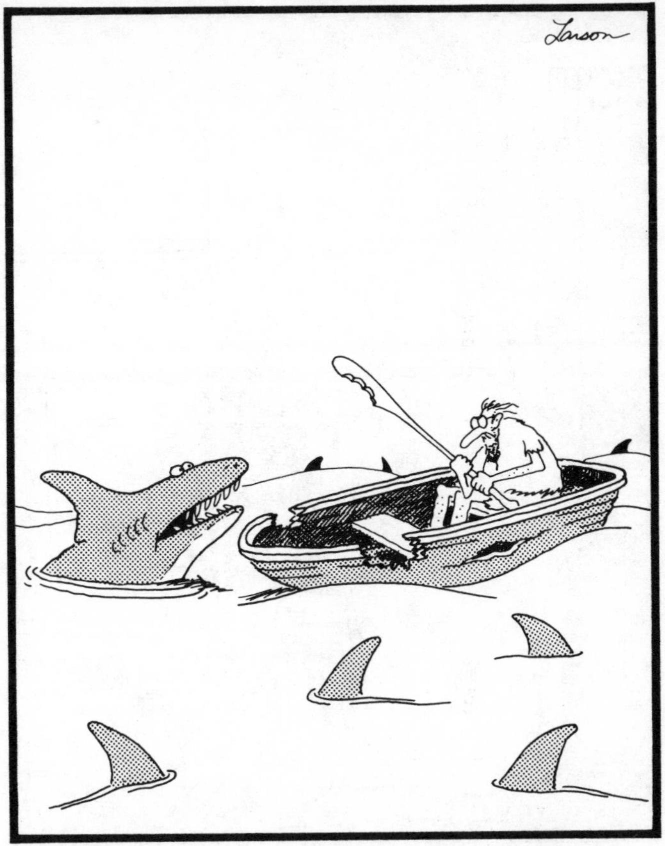

Larson

"Look. Why don't you just give yourself up quietly? . . . Otherwise, this thing could turn into a frenzy — and nobody wants that."

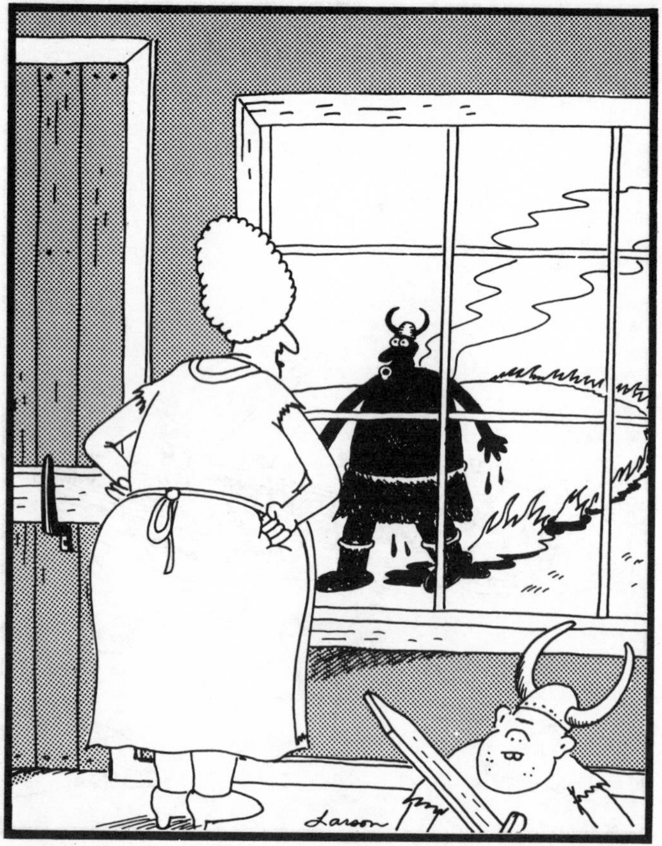
Larson

"Well, guess who's home a little early from today's castle siege?"

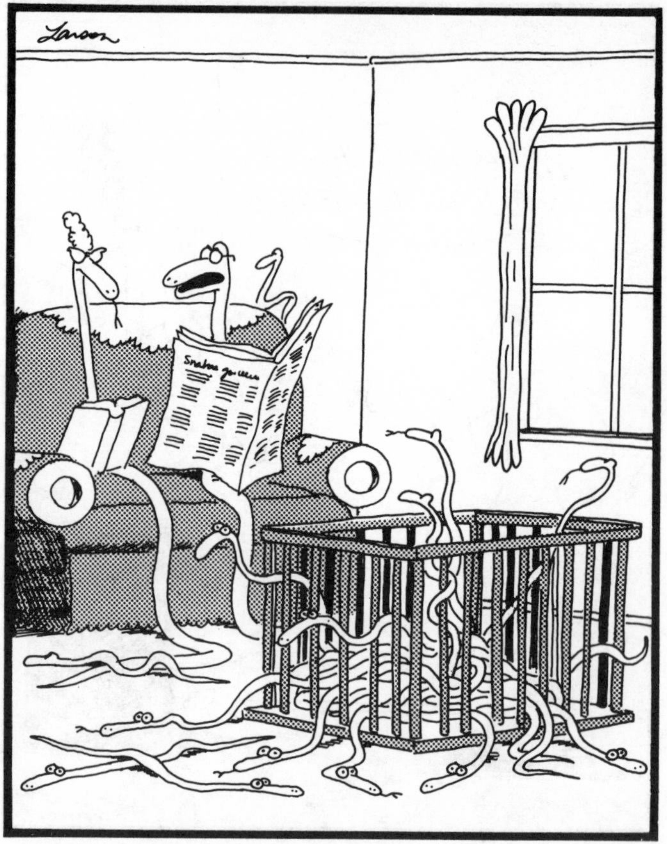
Larson

"I tell you, a crib is just plain worthless — what we need around here is a good cardboard box."

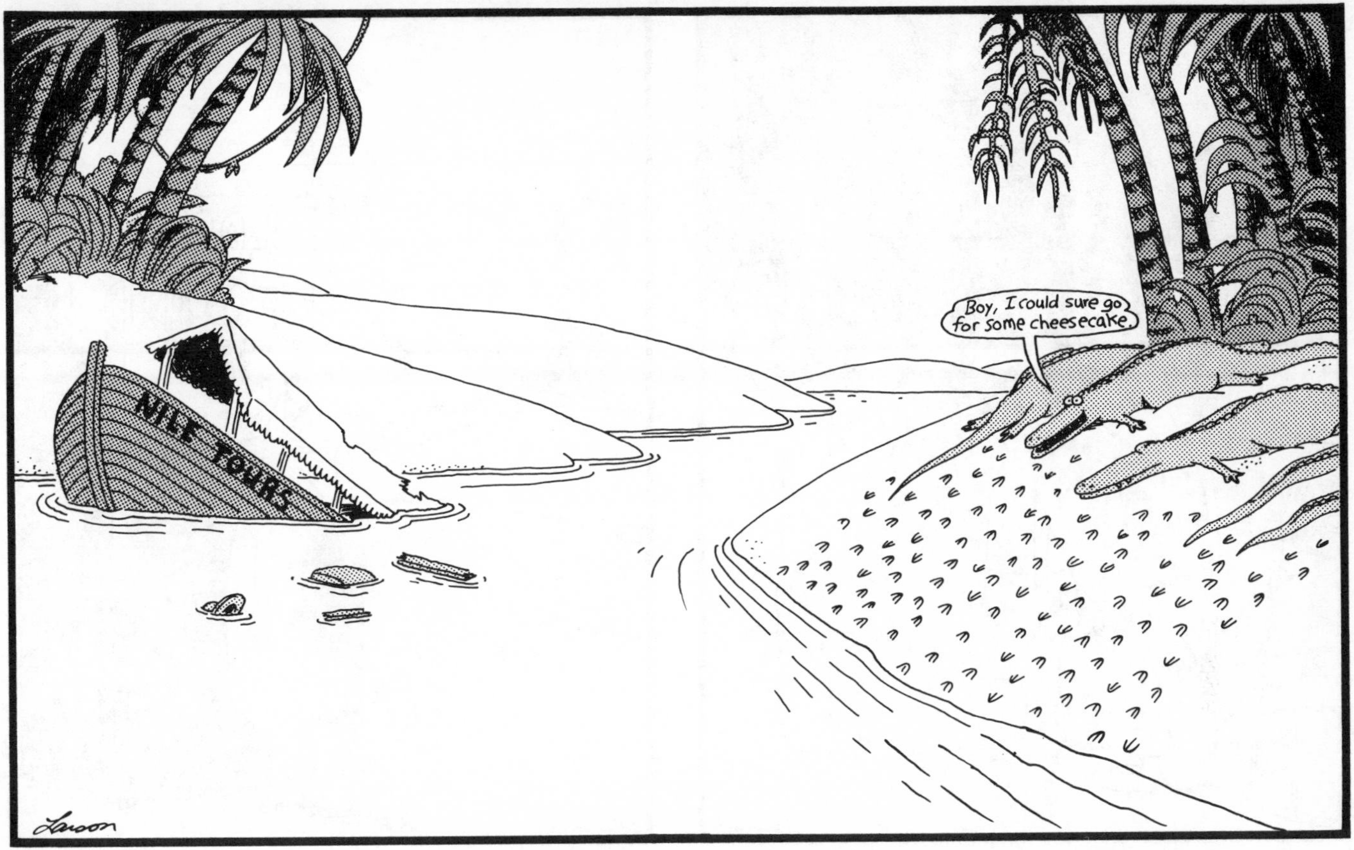
NILE TOURS
Boy, I could sure go for some cheesecake.
Larson

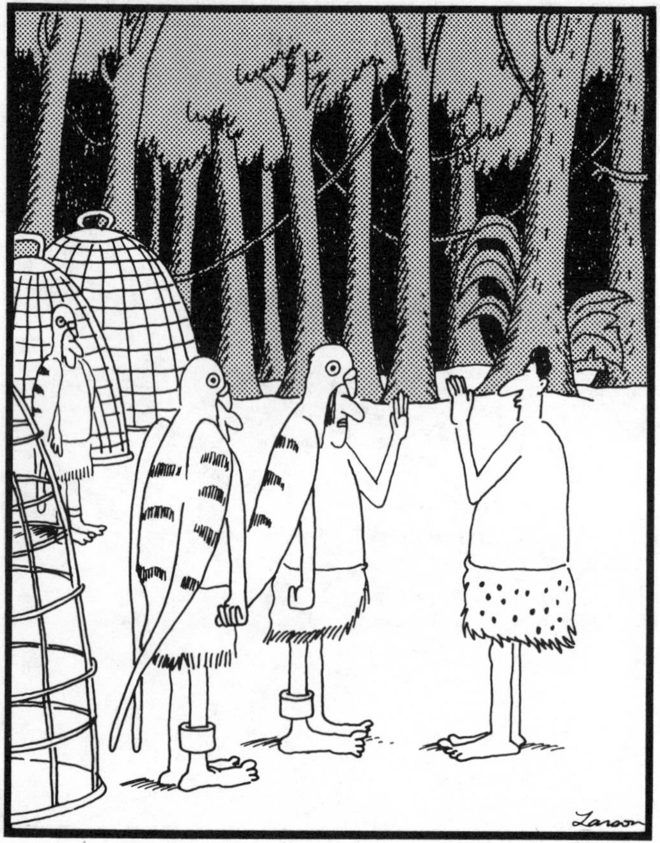
Larson

Tarzan is greeted by the Parakeet People.

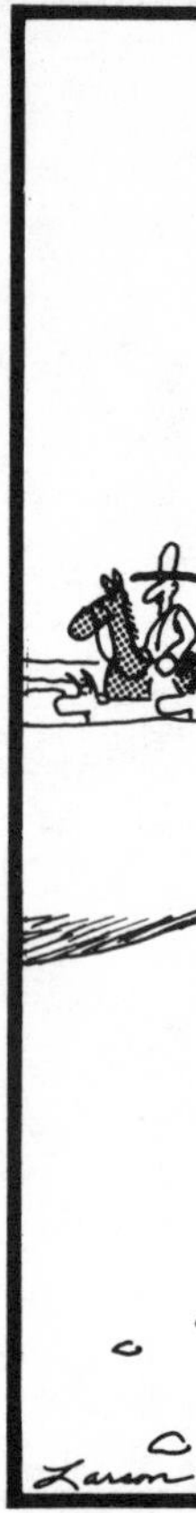
LOST &
FOUND
Larson

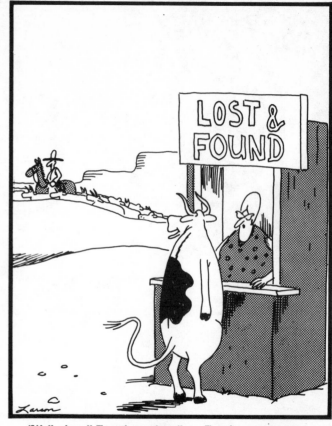

"Well, shoot! There's my herd! . . . Thank you anyway, ma'am."

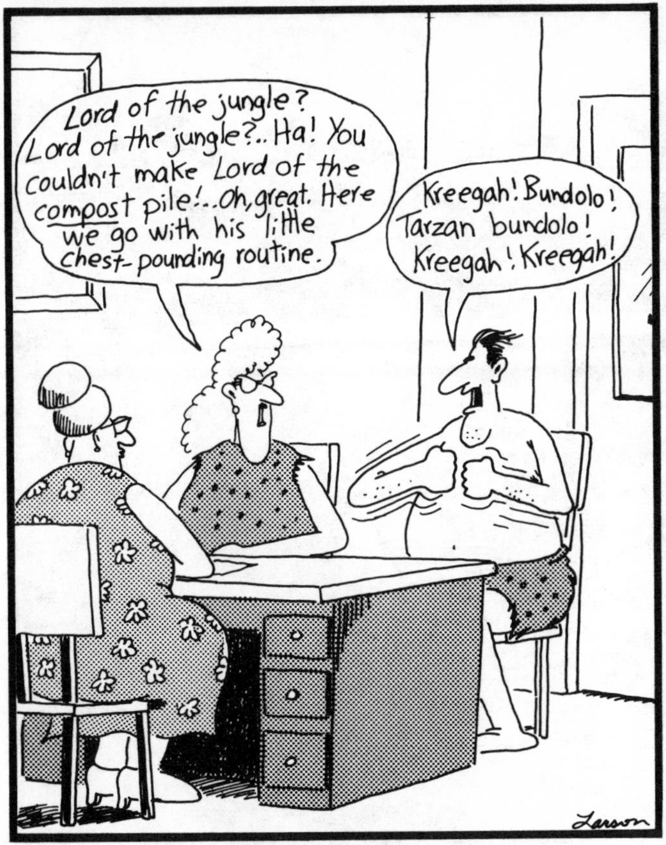
Lord of the jungle? Lord of the jungle?.. Ha! You couldn't make Lord of the compost pile!..Oh, great. Here we go with his little chest-pounding routine.
Kreegah! Bundolo! Tarzan bundolo! Kreegah! Kreegah!
Larson

The Greystokes at marriage counseling

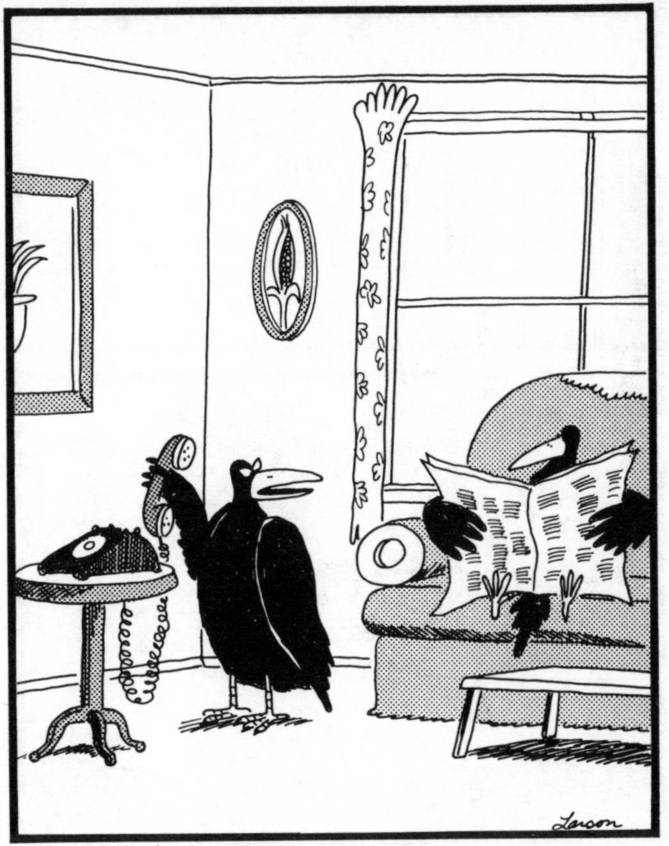
Larson

"Louis . . . phonecaw."

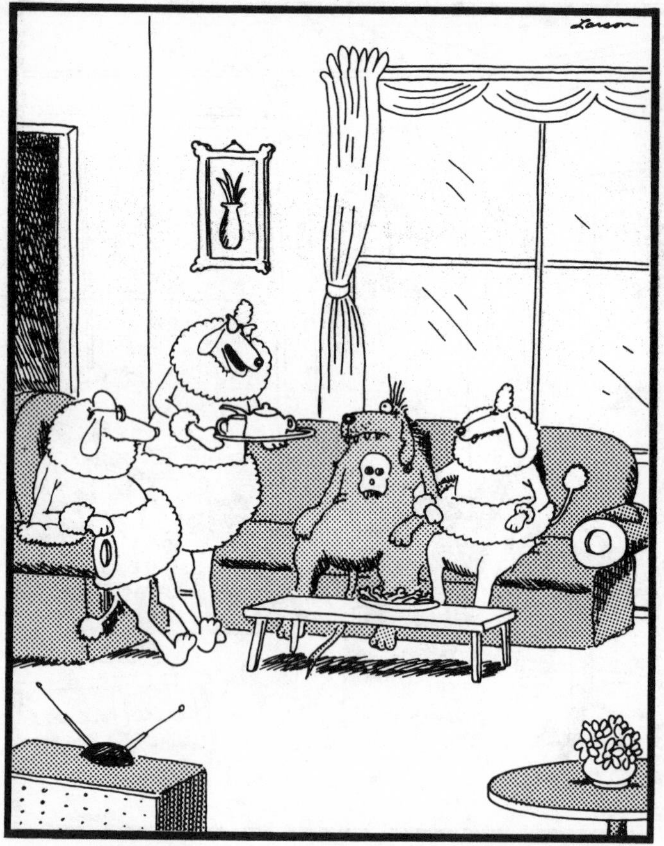
Larson

"So, Raymond . . . Linda tells us you work in the security division of an automobile wreckage site."

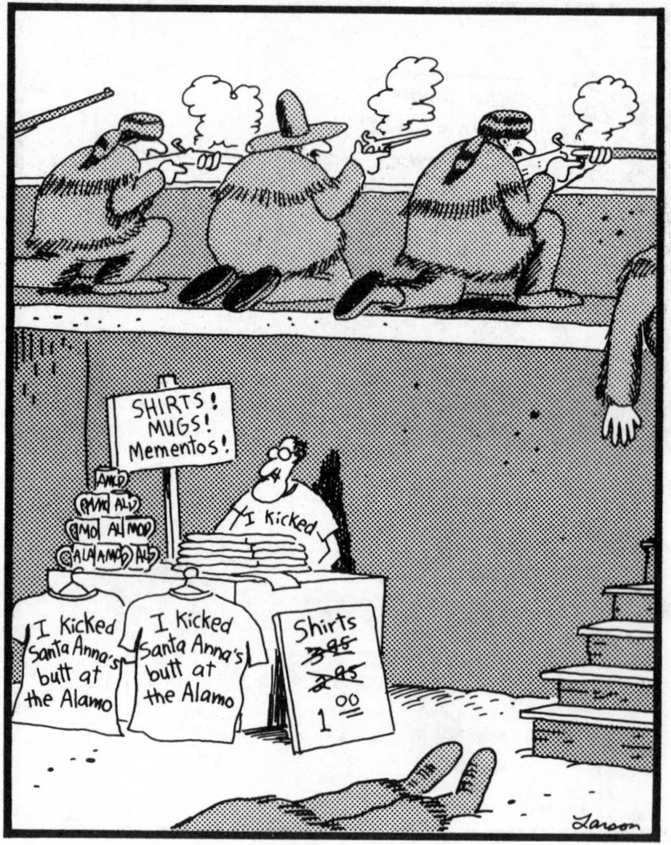
SHIRTS! MUGS! Mementos!
I Kicked
I Kicked Santa Anna's butt at the Alamo
I Kicked Santa Anna's butt at the Alamo
Shirts
1 00
Larson

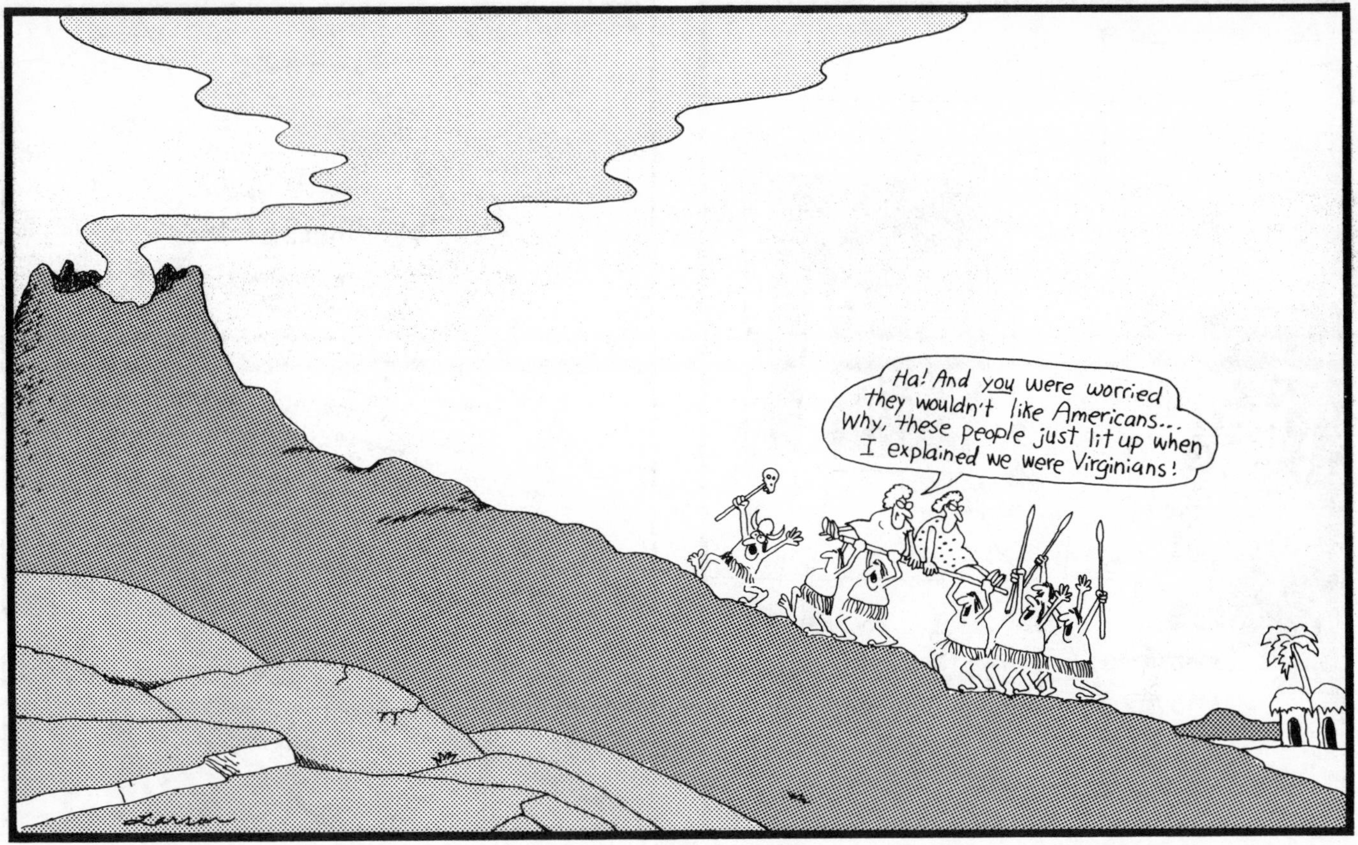
Ha! And you were worried they wouldn't like Americans... Why, these people just lit up when I explained we were Virginians!

SPIDER PERSONALS

BLACK WIDOW seeks male for fun weekends. 555-4688

BLACK WIDOW looking for nice male, same species 524888

BLACK WIDOW; attractive; large red hourglass, out-going. Call Susan 506-7186

BLACK WIDOW, fun-loving, attractive, long legs, wants to meet any male 555-1146

BLACK WIDOW, non-smoker seeks male to share indoor web. 555-0617

BLACK WIDOW, young, likes dark places to share w/so...

...WIDOW wants to meet male with no strings attach...

BLACK WIDO... wants to m...

BLACK WIDOW wants to meet a nice male who will...

BLACK WIDOW... for someone w... willing to shar...

BLACK WIDOW... male of same kit... for fun & gam...

BLACK WIDOW seeks someo... who willing... long walk...

BLACK W... if you'r... I'm...

SPIDER PE...

BLACK WIDOW enjoys going for long walk... and listening to...

BLACK WIDOW wa... to have a male cum... for quiet dinner an...

BLACK WIDOW...

In the early days, living in their squalid apartment, all three shared dreams of success. In the end, however, Bob the Spoon and Ernie the Fork wound up in an old silverware drawer, and only Mac went on to fame and fortune.

90

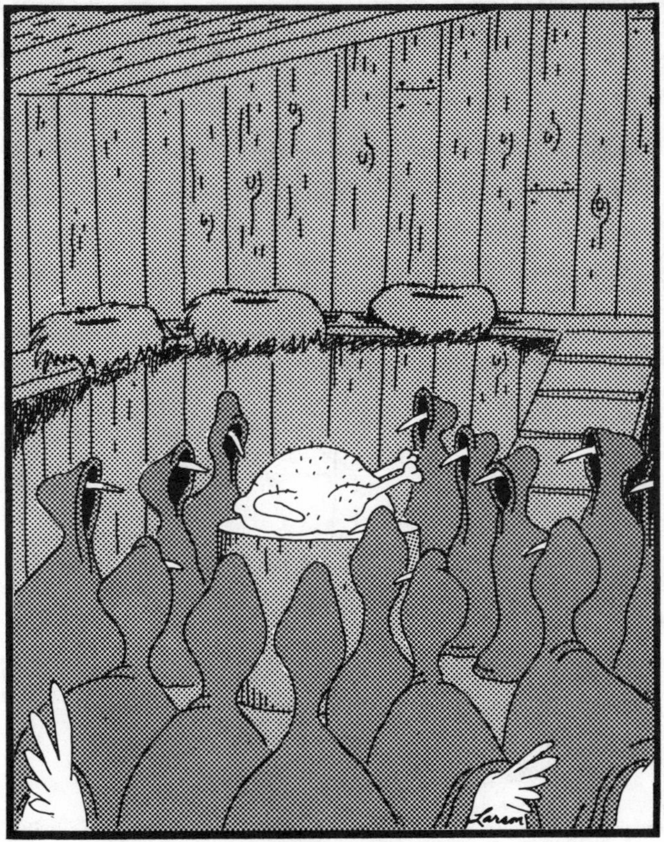
Larson

Chicken cults

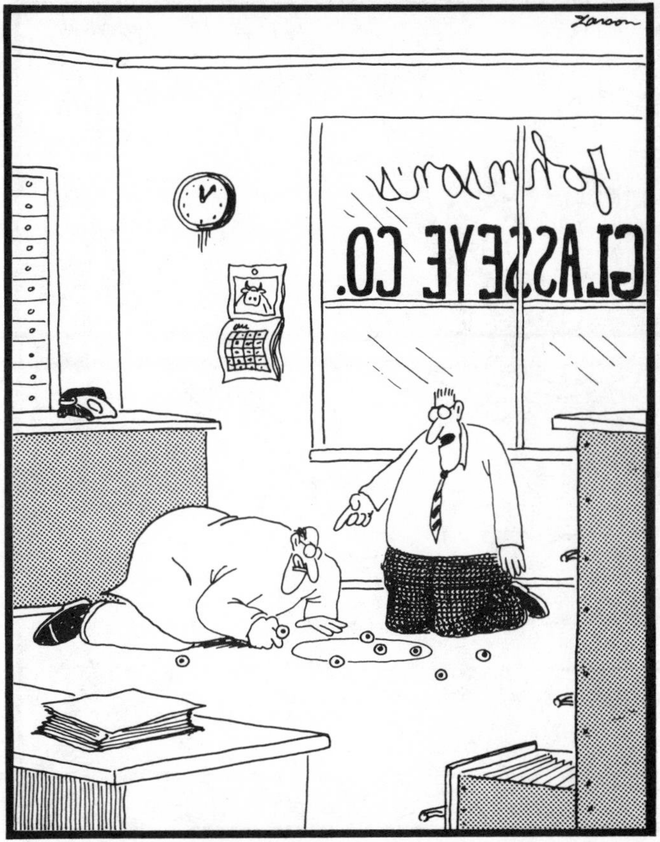
Larson
GLASSEYE CO.

"Just a word of warning, Myron — if you miss, I'm comin' after your big hazel."

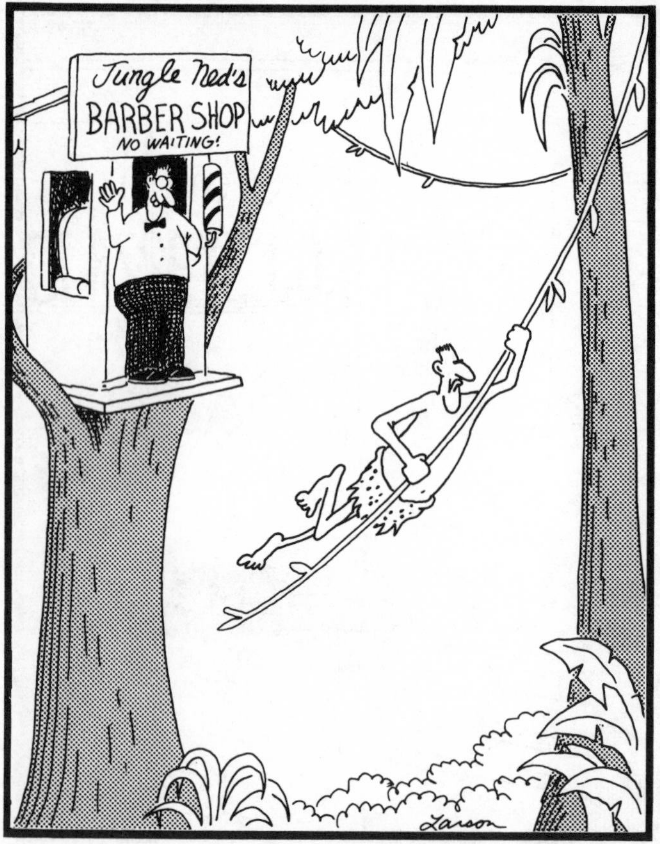
Jungle Ned's
BARBER SHOP
NO WAITING!

And for two excruciating months, he was simply known as "Skinhead of the Jungle."

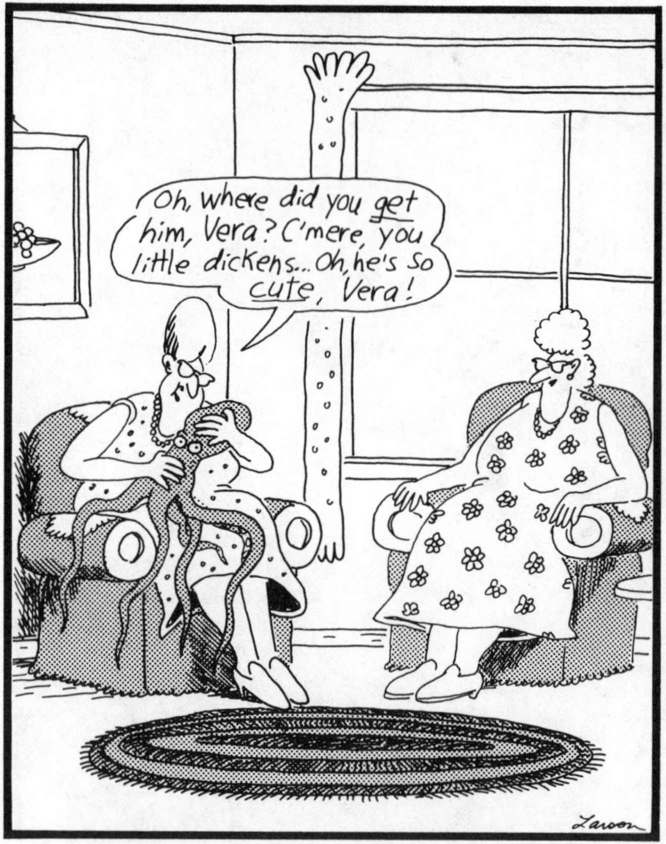
Oh, where did you get him, Vera? C'mere, you little dickens... Oh, he's so cute, Vera!

Seconds later, Mrs. Norton was covered with ink.

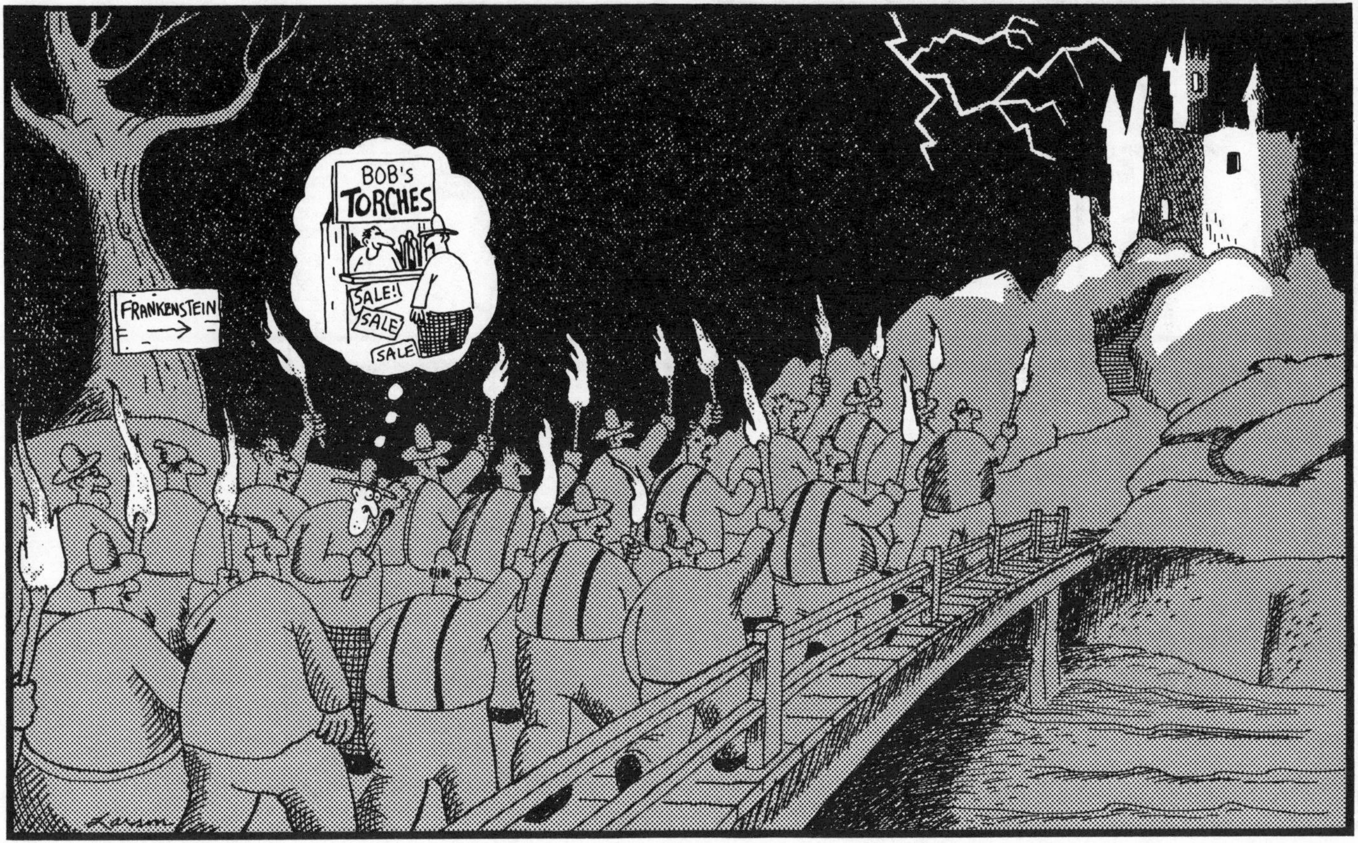
BOB's
TORCHES
SALE!!
SALE
SALE
FRANKENSTEIN

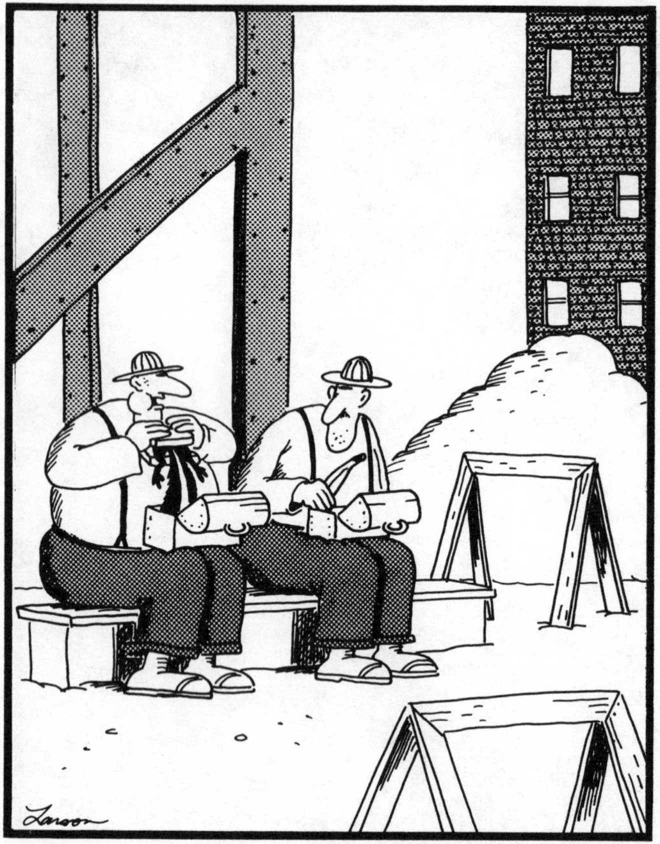
Larson

"Skunk sandwich, Bill . . . mmmmm . . . skunk sandwich. . . . Trade for that banana?"

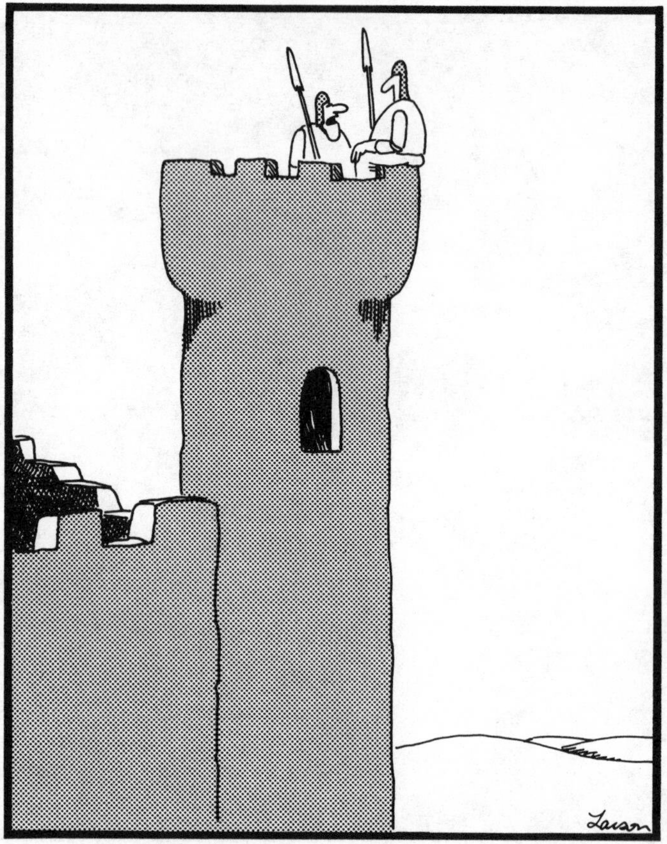
Larson

"Mom said no sitting on the edge, Wayne."

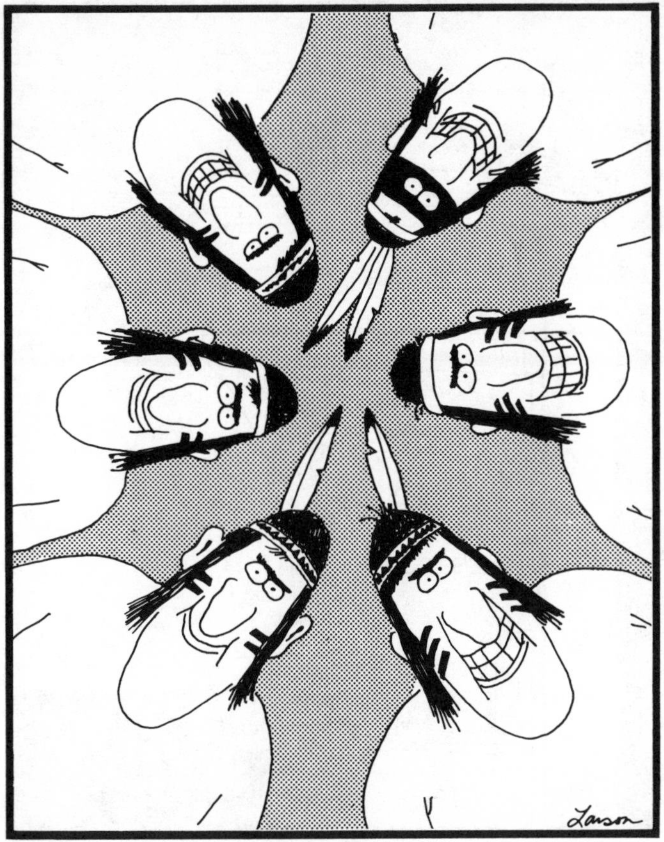
Larson

Custer's last view

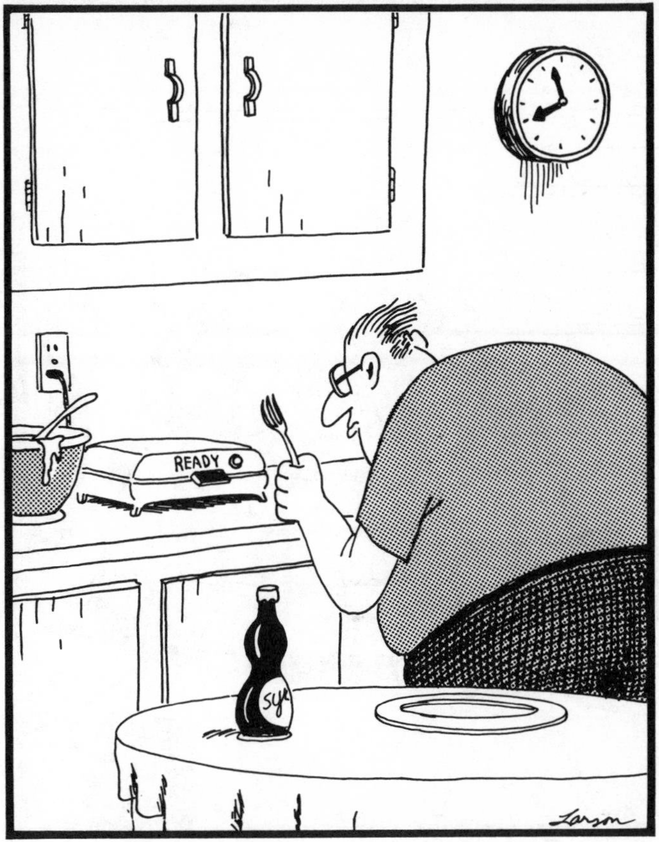
READY
Larson

Wendall Zurkowitz: Slave to the waffle light

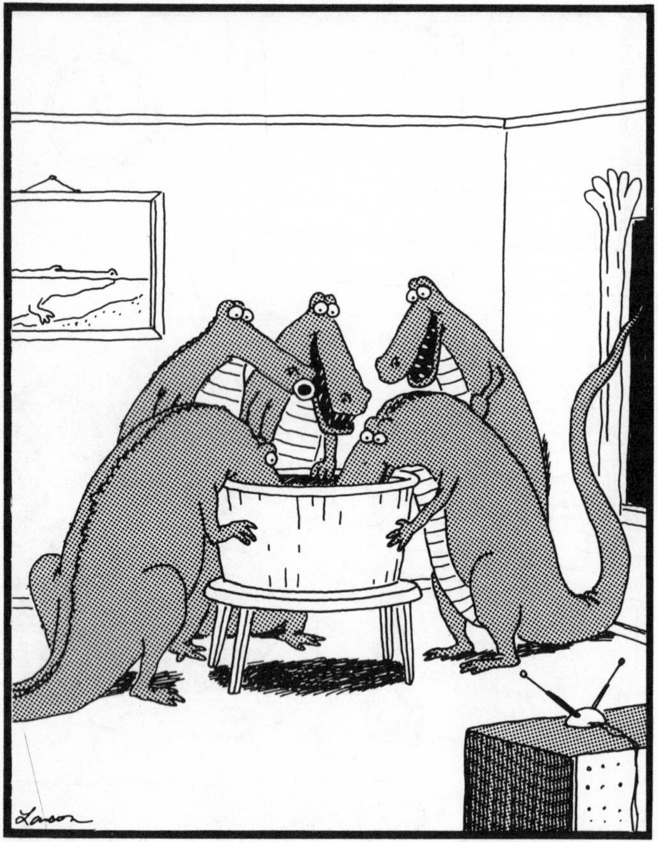
Larson

Bobbing for poodles

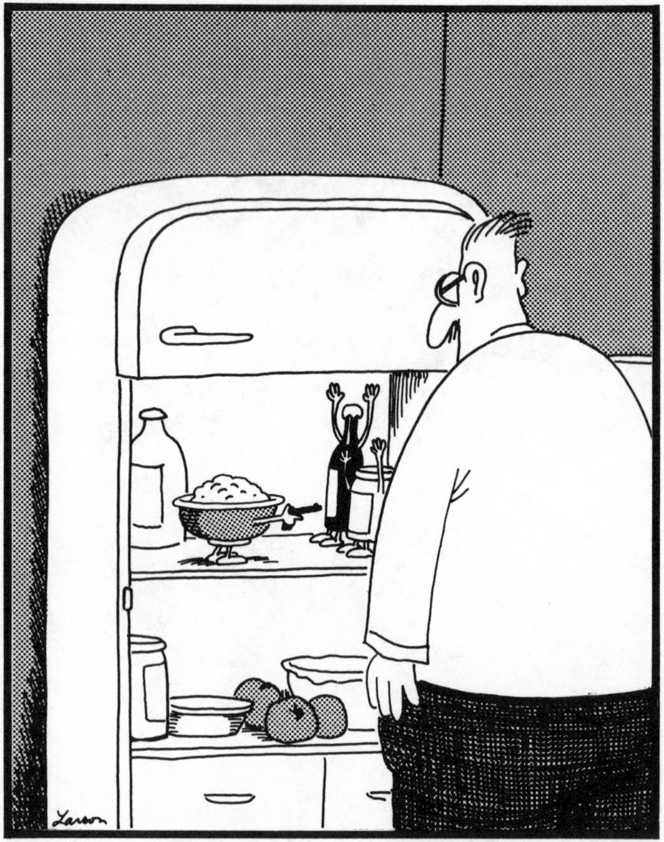
Larson

When potato salad goes bad

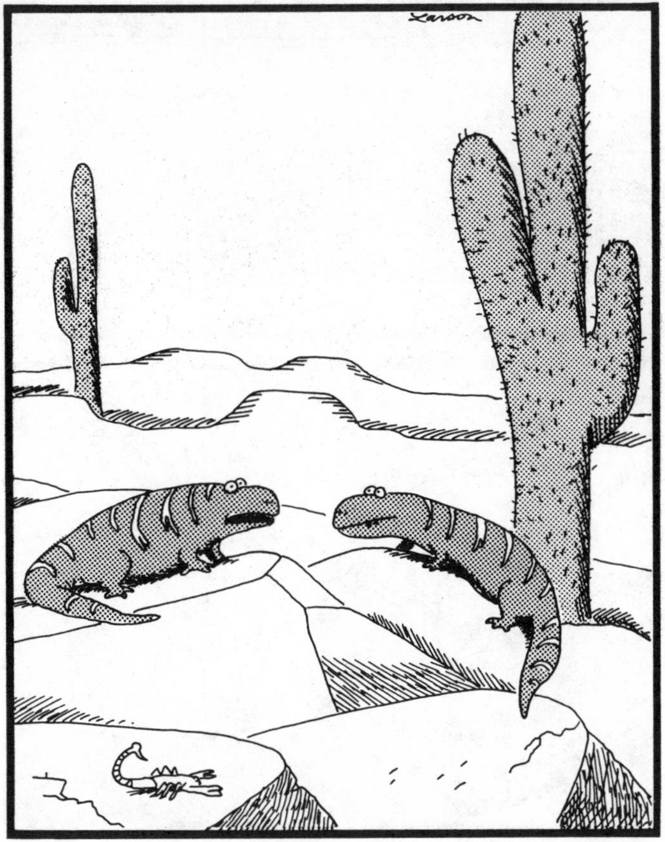
Larson

"There it is again . . . a feeling that in a past life I was someone named Shirley MacLaine."

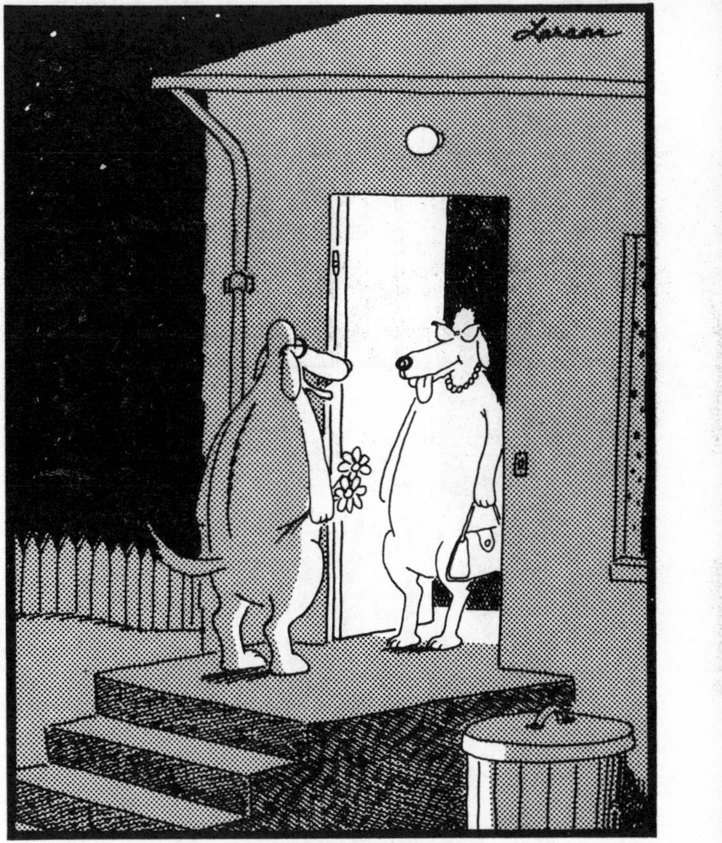
Larson

"Oh, Ginger — you look absolutely stunning . . . and whatever you rolled in sure does stink."

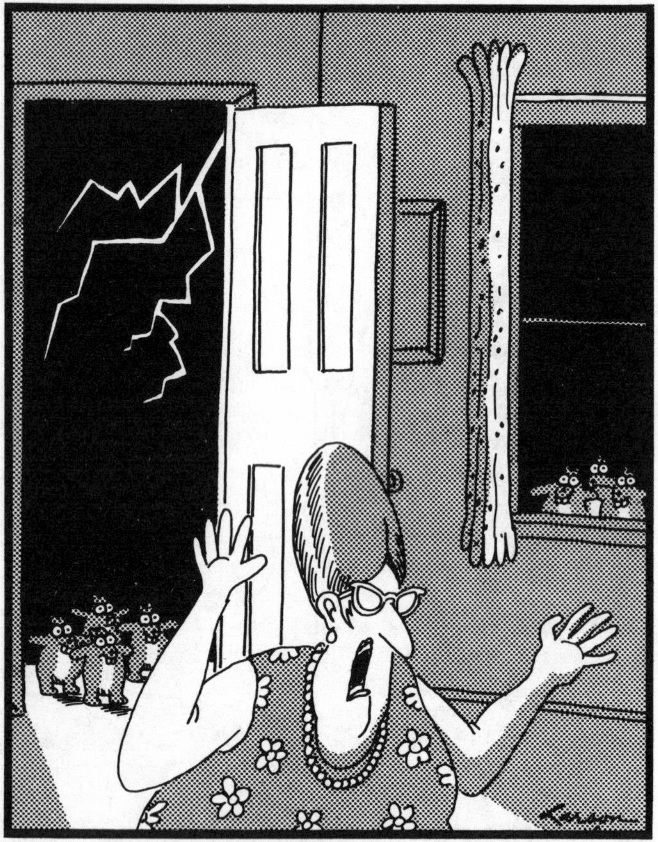

Night of the Living Dead Chipmunks

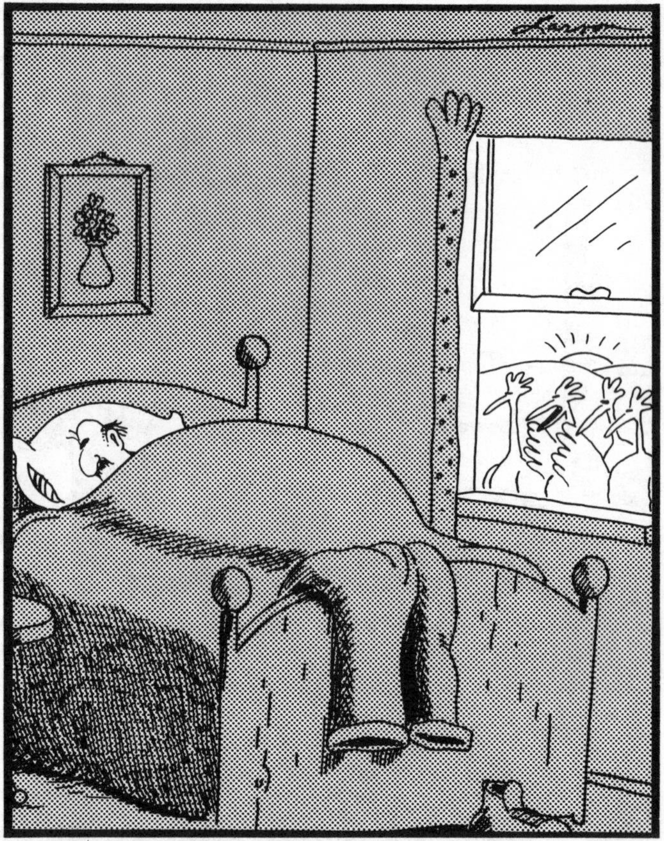

"Yo! Farmer Dave! Let's go, let's go, let's go! . . . You gettin' up with us chickens or not?"

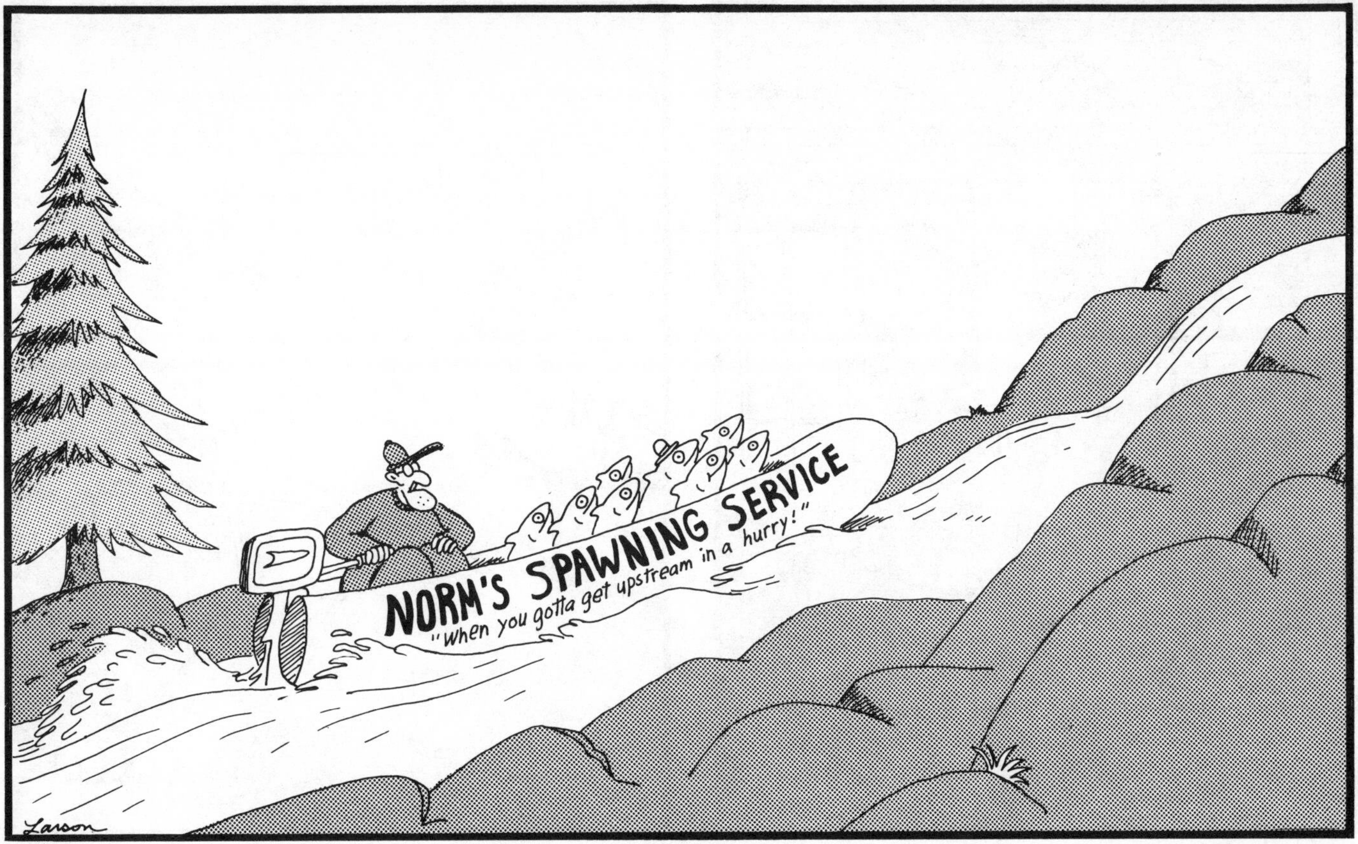
NORM'S SPAWNING SERVICE
"When you gotta get upstream in a hurry!"
Larson

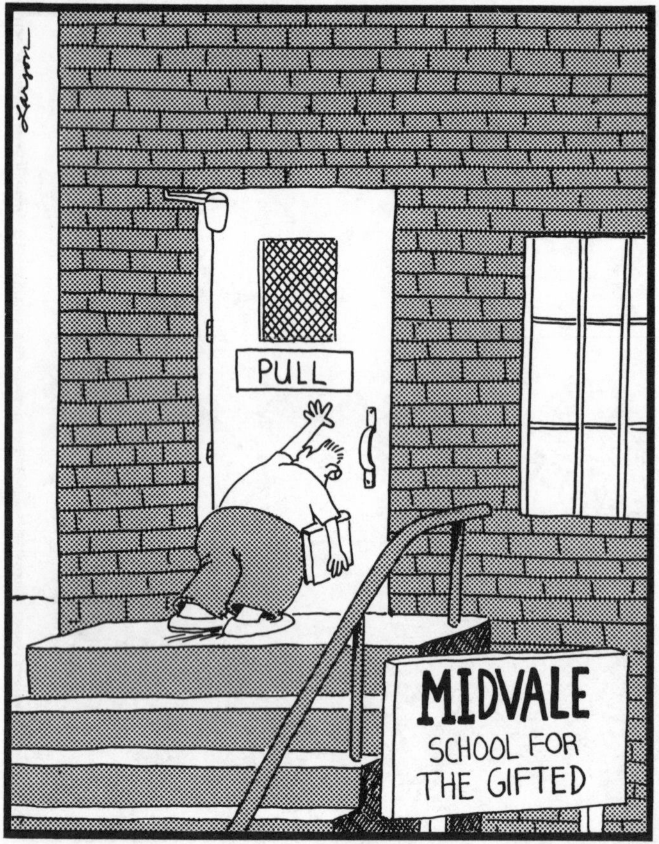
Larson
PULL
MIDVALE
SCHOOL FOR
THE GIFTED

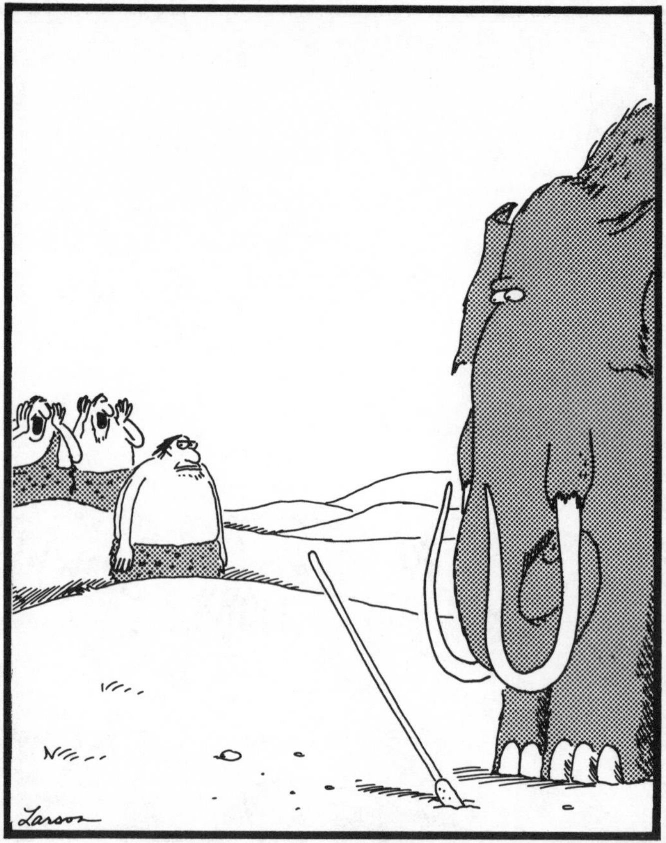
Larson

"Airrrrr spearrrr . . . airrrrr spearrrr! . . ."

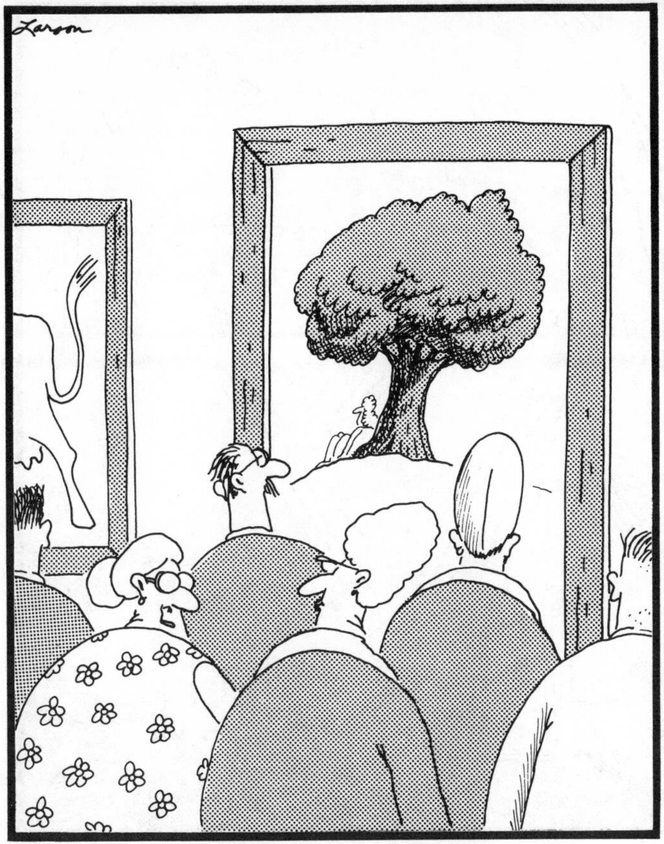

"My boy made the frame."

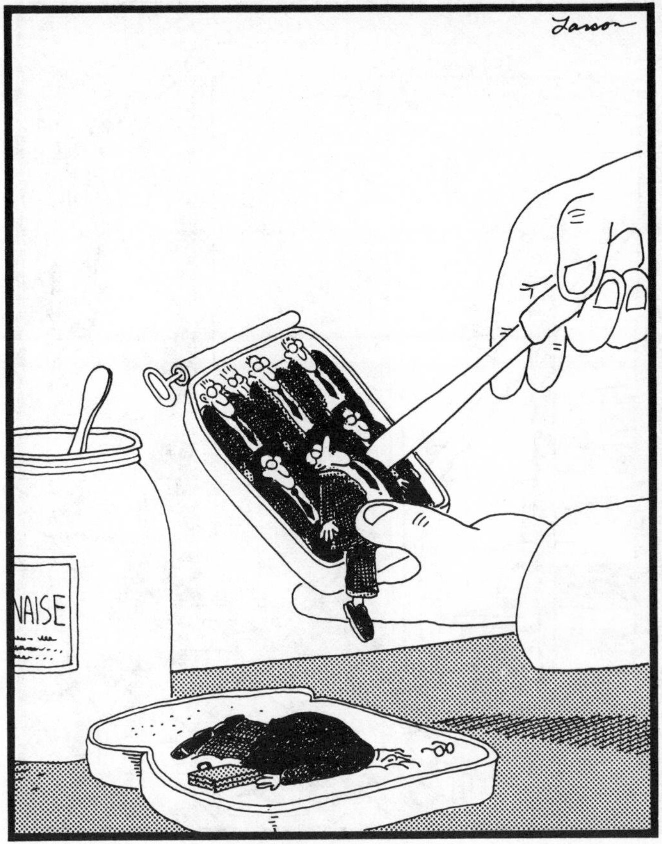
NAISE

Business lunch

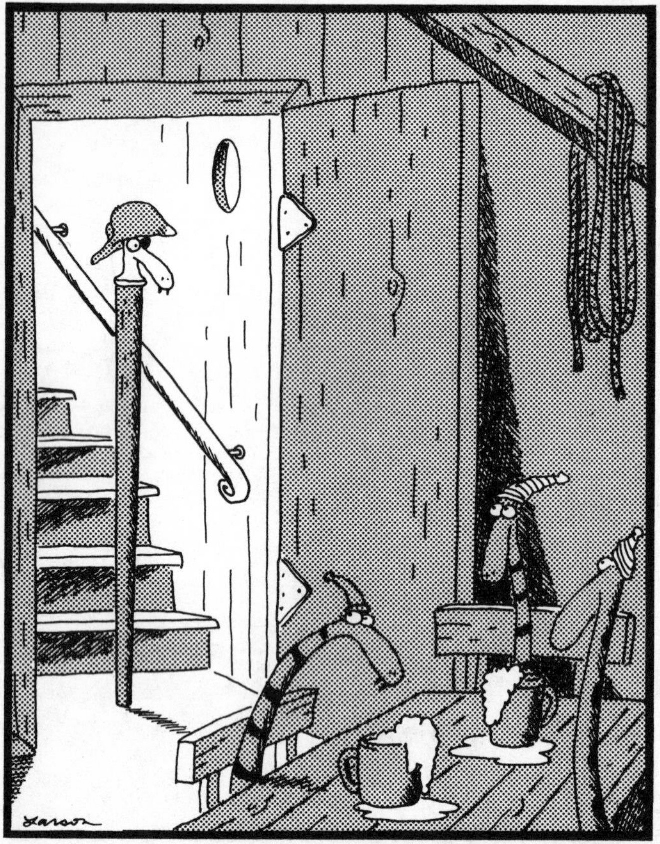
Larson

The door swung wide, and there, to the horror of the other pirates, stood Captain Monet — unmistakable with his one eye and pegbody.

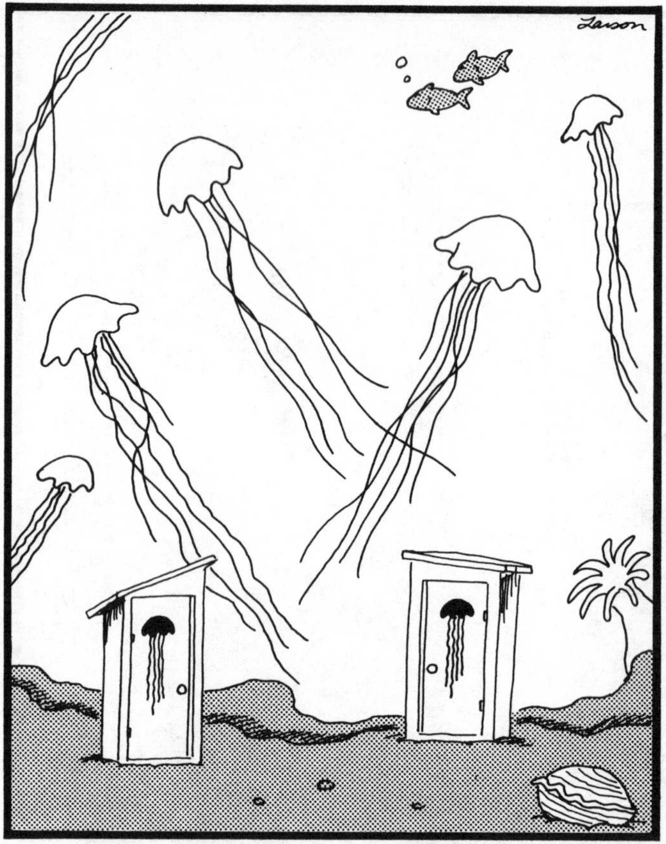
Larson

Only they know the difference.

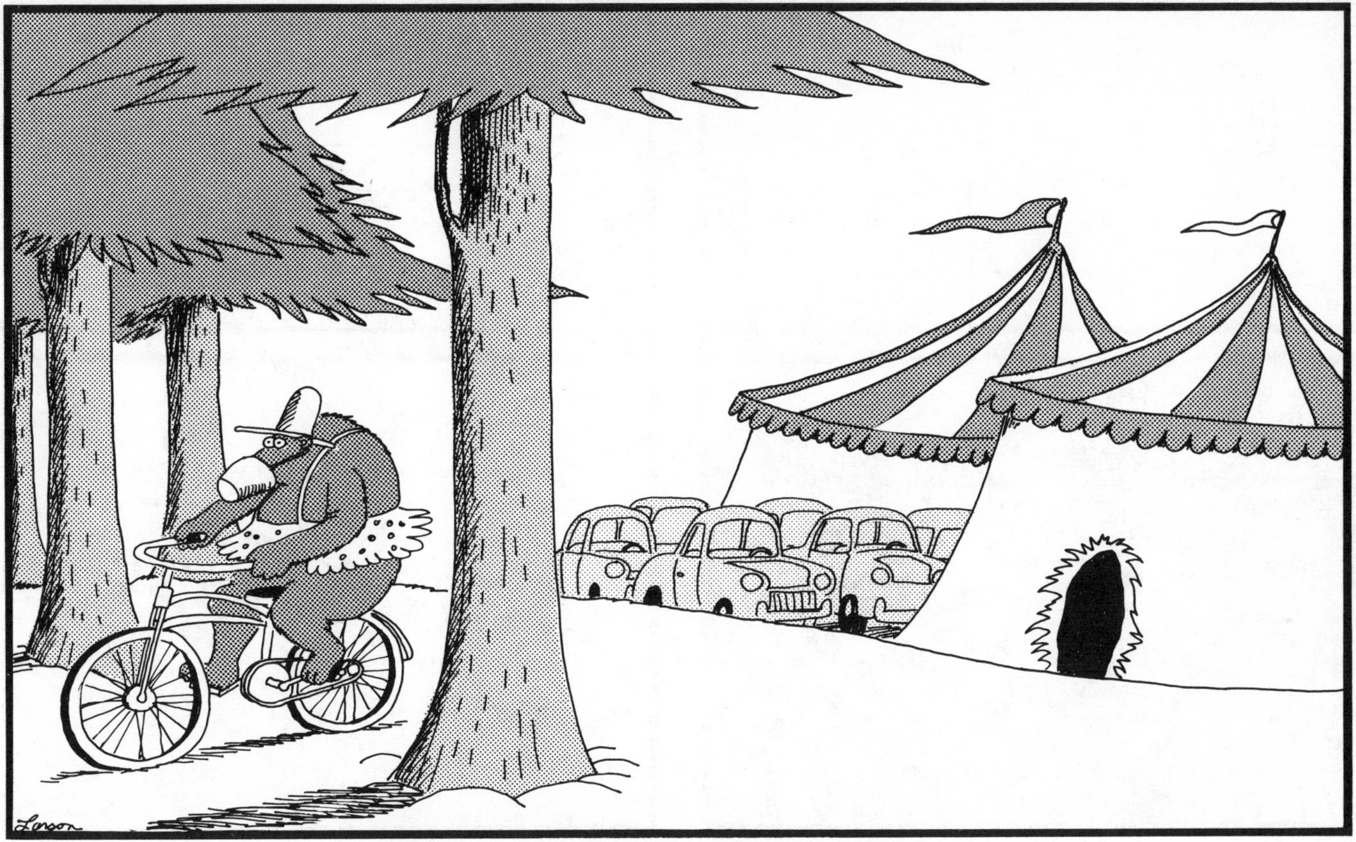
Larson

Bobo remained free the rest of his life, although he did find it necessary to seek counseling.

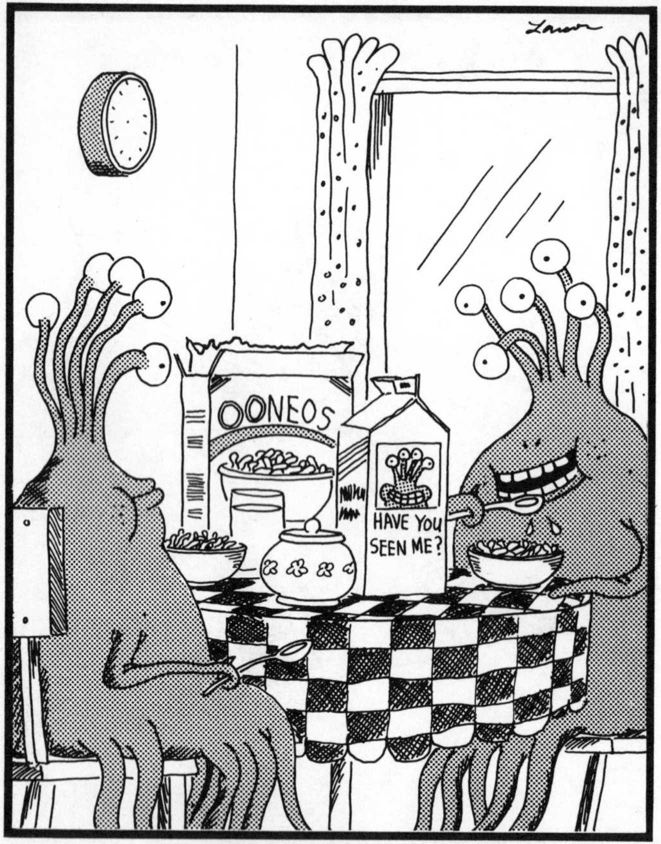
Larson
OONEOS
HAVE YOU
SEEN ME?

Breakfast on other planets

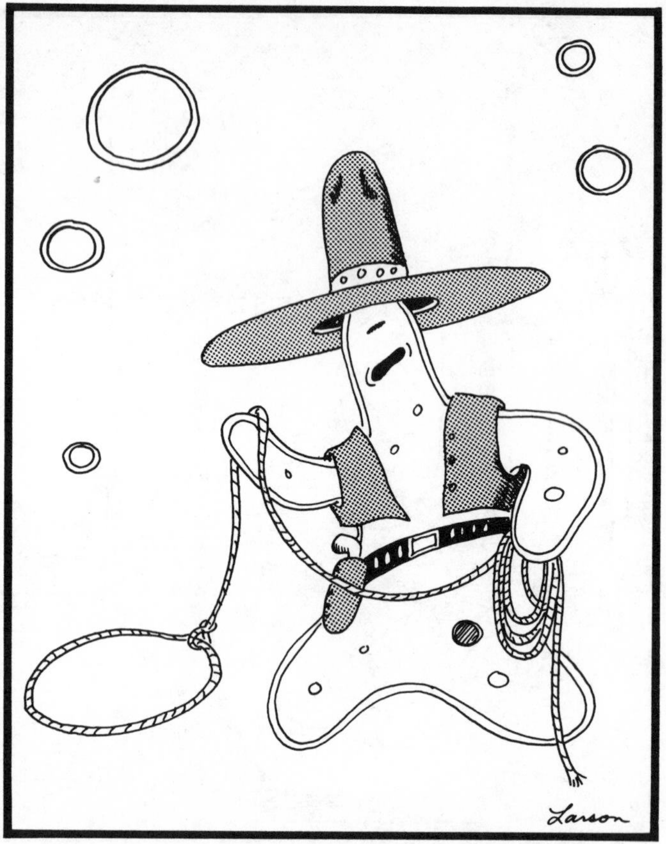
Larson

"So, until next week — Adios, amoebas."